James DeKoven

A Theological Defence for the Rev. James De Koven to the Council

Held at Milwaukee, February 11th and 12th, 1874

James DeKoven

A Theological Defence for the Rev. James De Koven to the Council
Held at Milwaukee, February 11th and 12th, 1874

ISBN/EAN: 9783337301125

Printed in Europe, USA, Canada, Australia, Japan

Cover: Foto ©Lupo / pixelio.de

More available books at **www.hansebooks.com**

A

THEOLOGICAL DEFENCE

FOR THE

REV. JAMES DE KOVEN, D.D.

WARDEN OF RACINE COLLEGE,

TO

The Council held at Milwaukee,

FEBRUARY 11th and 12th, 1874.

———⟶∙∙∙⟵———

RACINE, WIS.:

ADVOCATE STEAM PRINTING HOUSE AND BOOK BINDERY,
1874.

In Preface p. 2, for "civiley" read "civilly."

P. 24, for "Gorgoria" read "Gorgonia."

In Appendix p. 46, for "Alexader" read "Alexander."

P. 48 for "interrogaries" read "interrogatories."

P. 50 for "person" read "personal."

P. 52 for "p. 90" read "pp. 89 and 90."

P. 57 for "that" read "what."

P. 62 for prayer of Ignatius Loyola read:

> Anima Christi Sanctifica me
> Corpus Christi Salva me
> Sanguis Christi inebria me
> Aqua Lateris Christi lava me
> Passio Christi conforta me
> O bone Jesu exaudi me
> Intra tua vulnera absconde me, &c.

P. 63 for "*born*" read "*borne.*"

PREFACE.

The substance of the following defence was spoken to the Council held in Milwaukee, February 11th and 12th. I have omitted some few personal allusions that I might, so far as I could, wound the feelings of no one, and I have added certain things, which either haste, or excitement, or the exigencies of the occasion compelled me to omit, and have besides endeavoured to make the defence as full and complete as I could, without writing a theological treatise.

I am sure I may be pardoned for this, when I state that since the General Convention of 1871, with the exception of a correspondence between myself and the Rev. Dr. Craik of Kentucky, a brief correspondence published in the *Appendix to this Defence, and a note correcting a mistake in a matter of fact of the Rev. Dr. Andrews of Virginia; this is the only time I have ever published a word in my own defence.

My reasons for making my defence before the Council and for publishing it now are as follows:

a. Immediately after the General Convention of 1871 I was attacked in newspapers and elsewhere as an Idolater, and as one disloyal to the church.

b. At the Massachusetts Convention I was similarly attacked.

c. Since then by a series of misleading hints and dexterous misrepresentations in the Church Journal, I have been made to appear as the leader of a party in the church, and responsible for doctrines and views I do not hold, or upon which my judgement has never been expressed.

*See Appendix 1.

d. Churchmen of Massachusetts, some of them men venerable in years, and eminent for holiness of life and Christian labours, who, when one far better fitted than myself for the office of Bishop could not be nominated by them, did me the honour to give me their votes; have been also represented as mere partisans, the more to injure me.

e. The attacks in the Church Journal were followed up by repeated attacks in secular papers in Chicago and in Milwaukee.

f. Subjected in common with many of my brethren, clerical and lay, Dr. Kemper being of the number, to an interview with a reporter; and the last one waited on by him; I thought the best way, to meet what has come to be regarded as a licensed intrusion, was to answer as civiley and simply as I could. Stating, what I believe my defence has proved to be true, that the contest in this Diocese was not one of grave difference of principle; this was made the occasion for putting forth a document in order to disprove this assertion, and the sending it to the clergy and laity of the Diocese, and Bishops and Standing Committees all over the country; accusing me of doctrines I did not hold, and practices I did not practice. I was thereby arraigned by three Theological Professors of a well-known Theological Seminary before the whole Church.

g. All these things were known to be simply part of a crusade by an "aggressive and intolerant faction," chiefly without the Diocese, to brand men who could not utter the new Shibboleth which one or two Bishops had invented, as the sole test of sound Churchmanship; and to procure the practical condemnation of views which no competent ecclesiastical court would dare to condemn.

h. At the Council men came with speeches prepared against me, and things were said and done, which they who said and did them, must now profoundly regret.

i. Nominated for the office of Bishop on the last day of the Council, so far as I was concerned, it was no question of an Episcopal Election, but I was on trial before the Diocese and the whole land, as one disloyal to the Church of his Baptism.

j. I was placed in this difficulty. If I made no defence, it would have been justly said, what has been said about my previous silence, that I had none to make ; and when defeated, that I, and something more important—the doctrines I hold, had been condemned, not only by the popular voice, but by my brethren who knew me best, in my own Diocese. I could not leave the matter to my friends, for in matters of faith no one is content with a second-hand statement in a man's favour, though human nature is so constituted that it too readily accepts a second-hand statement against him. If I withdrew my name after I had been nominated, and then defended myself, the principle would have been established, that Church Newspapers, and Clergymen from without a Diocese, need only to send vehement accusing words into that Diocese, with sufficient frequency and dexterity; to secure the withdrawal of the name of the man they might choose to attack. Once grant that delicacy required this on the part of the person nominated, and a *veto power would practically be given to the editors of church newspapers* and to *any faction in the Church*, upon the free nomination of a Diocese; and if unresisted in this case, the attempt could be made elsewhere, and under other circumstances.

It has been said that there was no precedent for my action. This is not a correct statement.

In the General Convention of 1844, the election of Rev. Dr. Hawks to the Bishopric of Mississippi, came up for the canonical confirmation of the House of Clerical and Lay delegates. The election had passed through one stage indeed, but it was still undecided. Charges were made to the Lower House of General Convention against his moral character, and Dr. Hawks who was himself a delegate, defended himself in a speech of several hours to the Lower House. After a resolution had been passed declaring that his integrity had been vindicated, his election was not confirmed. I was myself present at a meeting of the Board of Trustees of the General Seminary when some twelve or thirteen Bishops and a very large company of distinguished Clergy and Laity had met together to act upon the nomination of the Rev. Dr. Mahan to the Professorship of Systematic Divinity. Dr. Mahan had been publicly accused, as I have been, of holding Romanizing views on the subject of Confession. Before the election, Dr. Mahan defended himself from these charges with his usual clearness and theological knowledge, and immediately afterwards, he was elected to this important position, all but one or at most two of the Bishops voting in his favour, and a large majority of Clergy and Laity.

But had there been no precedent I would have done the same. No such attack had ever before been made upon one nominated to the Episcopate. It was stated openly that it was not the person who was attacked but the views he held and the practices he practiced. Thus the occasion assumed an importance which lifted it far beyond all personal considerations.

When I spoke therefore, and to this I believe the heart of every true gentleman will beat responsive; it was for honesty and straightforward dealing, for the rights of my order and of every Churchman, for the truth of God and the faith of my forefathers. Not one moment bending to the storm, knowing that there was no possibility of my election; knowing too, what would be said of my action; but holding these precious rights beyond all false delicacy, I spoke ; and had I been silent, I had been thrice a coward.

For the same reason, I print it and send it forth, asking those who think kindly of me to give it a patient reading, and those who have doubted or thought ill of me, in the quiet calm of this holy season, to weigh words, which, if they do not con-vince, are at least sincere.

Racine College, Lent, 1874.

Mr. President, and Brethren of the Council:

I really do not think, after all that has been so kindly said in my behalf, and in view of the feeble character of the attacks upon me, that I need to vindicate myself. I do not feel that I need to convince to-day any honest-hearted man, in this House, that I have been most gravely misrepresented. I would leave the whole matter just as it is, content with your unspoken verdict, were it not for one thing. It is not for Wisconsin alone, and for these kind friends whom years have only bound the closer to me, that I speak. I am arraigned to-day before the whole Church of the United States of America. This document, full of cruel accusations, signed by six Presbyters of this Diocese, has been sent all over this Diocese. It has been also sent outside of this Diocese, and has thus been scattered far and wide. It is not a question of the election to the Episcopate. That is immaterial, and is in the hands of God. The question is, as to whether I am an honest, loyal clergyman of the Church, or one who professing to be so, teaches doctrines she denies, and inculcates practices she forbids.

In addition to this, I am placed by God's providence at the head of a Church College. Its only claim to exist, and to receive the loving favour with which it has been blessed, is, that it loyally represents the Godly discipline, and Christian nurture, which have been for generations the especial glory of our mother Church. That it is a Church College, Catholic not Protestant, Protestant not Roman, has been the one thing that has commended it. If the charges of my brethren are true, I have no right to be at the head of it. Nay; how can he who is false himself, train gentle children and brave young men, in manly honour? Take notice also, that the Rt. Rev. Dr. Cummins has accused me of enforcing confession upon the students. His poor band of ministers, in every sermon, now at Chicago, now at Detroit, now at Peoria and St. Louis, and I know not where else, have even given as one justification of their schism, that enforced confession prevails at Racine College. This might be borne. One could reasonably hope that loyal Churchmen might love the more a Priest, whom the enemies of the Church saw fit to speak evil of.

The *Church Journal* also, by dexterous insinuations and misleading hints, has left impressions which, while quite incorrect, it could easily say it had never expressed in so many words. By refusing to admit a defence, which another kindly sent, it was made to seem as though no answer could be made. Some anonymous correspondent had called me a "standard bearer," and thus it was made to appear as if I maintained every view and practise, which any ritualist of any sort, or any society of ritualists might have held, from the publication of the first tract for the Times, down to the last issue of the *Church Times*. Mr. President, I am the "standard bearer," if you will, of every truth the Prayer Book teaches, and of none others. I am responsible for every word I have myself uttered; and for every statement of doctrine I have myself made; but for none besides. Be they true or false, no man can justly hold me responsible for them.

Under all this, too, lies a great principle. The Church has provided proper safeguards if a Diocese selects a person unfitted for the high office of Bishop. But sad will be the day, if before an Episcopal election, Church papers can feel that they may become campaign documents, and Clergymen think it their duty to send into a mourning Diocese, bitter accusing words of some one of their Brethren.

But in addition to this I am accused by six of my brethren, in my own Diocese, among my own people. Believe me when I say, that grievously wronged as I have been, I have no unkind feelings toward these gentlemen. I think, as I have said, that they have been wrong and done me wrong. Some of them I fancy begin to feel it. They cannot have clear consciences about it. One of them, indeed, (the Rev. Mr. Parke) has withdrawn his name and expressed his sorrow for signing it. But, and here is the difficulty, just in proportion as the virtue, and honour and venerable character of some of these gentlemen are believed in, in that proportion is the paper the heavier charge against me. With two of them, Dr. Adams and Dr. Kemper, I have had a friendship of twenty years, interrupted, I know, by an occasional disagreement, but still, so far as I am concerned, without the loss, until this sad occasion, of honest regard for them. This document goes out to the Church strengthened by their supposed friendship and long knowledge of me, and by every virtue that they possess. And it is just so much more of a charge against me, and makes it so much the more imperative upon me that I should defend myself.

I hope however that my Brethren will remember, that I have never made a statement on the doctrine of the Eucharist except the one I made in the general Convention of 1871, and afterwards in a correspondence which took place between myself and the Rev. Dr. Craik, of Kentucky. The other matters which have been spoken of, in the course of the speeches, but which are not mentioned in the document, took place earlier still, before the meeting of that general Convention. These false doctrines of mine, if they be false, and these wrong practices, if they be wrong, have been held and known for at least three years, and yet this is the first time they have thought it proper publicly to take me to task for them. At their ordination these gentlemen promised " with all faithful diligence to banish and drive away from the church all erroneous and strange doctrines contrary to God's word." The church provides a definite way for them to do this. If I have ever held or taught some of the views, mentioned in this document, I am liable to prosecution for false doctrine. And, Mr. President, if any Presbyters will come forward and present me for false doctrine on the ground that I hold what is taught in that document, I am ready to bear my trial, and will put no obstacles in their way. This is the legiti-mate way ; but to wait until the question of the Episcopate comes up, and then to circulate a series of charges against me, in such a way too, that I cannot defend myself, this is to be an accuser of one's Brethren, and to do that which all honourable men must condemn.

And now let me say that I have no wish to hide from any member of the council, or any man or woman in this diocese, just what I hold and just what I do. There are some things that are true in this paper. If it had been all false, it would not have been so effective. It is the skill of the document, that it mingles the false and the true, and so mingles them that the unskilled man would not be able to distinguish them. It is so dexterously arranged, that I have no hesitation in saying that the majority of laymen who have come to the council, have come believing me to be a Romanizer, because of this document. I therefore take up, and propose to examine the paper entitled,

"PRINCIPLES NOT MEN."*

First I must call your attention to the note which the six Presbyters have signed ; they say " *They have seen an article in the Milwaukee papers of Jan. 31st,*" which they reprint. And yet Dr. Egar, one of the signers of this note, has told us on this floor, *that he himself was the author of the anonymous article.* In a matter so grave as an accusation against a fellow Presbyter, and in defence of what they must call the truth, does this seem altogether sincere? They speak of it as a thing they had accidentally seen, as though they had not known who the author was, and all about it. It is a sort of thing which is sometimes done I am aware ; but scarcely with clean hands and pure lips.

Second, let me call your attention to the first and second paragraphs of the document. It does not say in so many words, but it carefully insinuates that the "interview" between myself and others with the reporter of the *Times* was the result on my part of "previous instructions." The statement of the charge will be, I think, to those who know me, its own refutation. I made every effort to avoid the "interview," and if it seemed to be favorable to me, I will venture to suggest, that this was due not to political chicanery on my part, but to the fact that the truth was on my side.

Third, I beg to call your attention to the question of

THE "PHILLIMORE JUDGEMENT."

In the general Convention of 1871, a new Canon on the subject of Ritual was proposed, to which in common with many of my Brethren I was earnestly opposed. The discussions upon the subject almost necessarily brought up the question of the Eucharist. Men upon the floor of the house,

*See Appendix ii.

had uttered very low views upon this important subject. I felt it my duty, boldly to state a view of the Eucharist, which the church allowed, and which I myself held.

The Court of Arches, (which while not the highest court of appeal in England, has nevertheless been regarded as the highest ecclesiastical court, because it is the Archbishop's court, though a lay Judge presides in it, as his "official Principal,") had tried and given sentence in the case of Mr. Bennett. Mr. Bennett on conscientious grounds had refused to appear either personally or by counsel, and thus was totally undefended. In spite of this, Sir Robert Phillimore, the Judge of the Court of Arches, had decided that the words " the real actual presence of our Lord under the form of bread and wine upon the altars of our churches," and "who myself adore, and teach the people to adore Christ present in the elements under the form of bread and wine," "did not contravene the formularies of our Faith." He said, " If I were to pronounce that they did so, I should be passing sentence in my opinion, upon a long roll of illustrious Divines, who have adorned our Universities, and fought the good fight of our church, from Ridley to Keble—from the Divine whose martyrdom the cross at Oxford commemorates, to the Divine in whose honour the University has founded her last College." [Phillimore Judgement, pp. 133 and 134.]

The case was carried up on appeal to the Judicial Committee of the Privy Council, a court without the slightest claim to the name of ecclesiastical, and which was so poorly constituted that it has within the past year, in the shape in which it existed at the time spoken of, been abolished by Parliament. It is quite true that some of the Bishops might sit as Privy Councillors, and the judgement of the council was written, it is said, by the Archbishop of York. The judgement was given June 8th 1872, more than six months after the general Convention. But, and here is the point, though Mr. Bennett was again undefended by counsel the Judicial Committee were compelled *to acquit him.* In other words both courts decided that the words of Mr. Bennett could be used, and such views be held by a Priest of the Church of England, and not contravene the formularies of the faith. It makes no difference, that the Archbishop of York should have indulged in the

Judgement in some harsh epithets. The Judgement of the Judicial Committee states distinctly, "It is not the part of the Court of Arches nor of this Committee, to usurp the functions of a Synod or of a Council. Happily their duties are much more circumscribed, namely whether certain statements are so far repugnant to, or contradictory of, the language of the articles and formularies, construed in their plain meaning, that they should receive judicial condemnation." [Judgement of Judicial Committee, p. 303, in the argument of A. J. Stephens, Q. C. &c.] Everything therefore in it, or in the Judgement of the Court of Arches, which went beyond the acquittal of Mr. Bennett, rests upon its own merits. The acquittal remains, the rest are *obiter dicta*. I must object here to Dr. Adams' style of reasoning, which because I have adopted certain "adjudicated words," makes me responsible for everything Mr. Bennett may have said in his "Plea for Toleration." I am of course responsible for every word of Mr. Bennett's I have adopted, but for none other.

The words were really, however, the words of Dr. Pusey rather than of Mr. Bennett, and they were quoted by me as the decision of a Judicial Tribunal, and cannot be so used as to involve me in any other expressions of the party on trial. They are quoted as the lawyer or the Judge when appealing to authority cites a legal decision. This is a principle too plain to need further enforcement. This will serve also to explain the fact that I did not even quote Mr. Bennett's words, which were "*in the sacrament*," not "*in the elements*." I was quoting a judicial decision and took it as it was.

This statement will serve to correct a mistake into which many have fallen. In the first edition of the "Plea for Toleration," Mr. Bennett used expressions which cannot be defended. In the third edition he substituted for them the phrases "the real actual Presence of our Lord under the form of bread and wine upon the Altars of our Churches," and "who myself adore and teach the people to adore Christ present in the *Sacrament* under the torm of bread and wine." For these expressions he was tried. Sir Robert Phillimore in his judgement substituted for *Sacrament* the word *Elements* and adjudicated these words. He probably did so because in Mr. Bennett's use and in Sir Robert Phillimore's judgement the words are precisely equivalent. They are not necessarily equivalent, but in the present case they were so. Mr. Stephens in his argument against Mr. Bennett, before the Judicial Committee, also regards them as equivalent. But whether this be so or not is immaterial to my argument, for I was quoting not Mr. Bennett's or Dr. Pusey's words, but a judicial decision, and so was bound, of course, to give the very words of that decision, which I did in the General Convention, quoting directly from it, and which I do now. It must also be remembered that the judgement of the Judicial Committee, from which people generally quote, gives Mr. Bennett's words exactly, but as this judgement was not given until more than six months after the General Convention, it was impossible for me to quote it.

My own view of the Presence I have expressed throughout the present "defence" by the words "in sacramental union with the consecrated elements," which expresses what I mean by "in the elements," and guards against a danger to which those words are possibly, though not necessarily exposed. They show, what I have always maintained, that the Presence in the Elements is not a material, but a spiritual and Sacramental Presence. Therefore in using the words of the " Phillimore Judgment" I did so with the most careful explanation. I said they were words " bolder and barer than any I would use except in a company of theologians." I declared that I did not believe in Transubstantiation. I asserted that the Presence in the Holy Elements was not material or carnal, but *spiritual.* I even went so far as to add something to the words of the judgement, using instead of "who myself adore and teach my people to adore Christ present in the elements under the form of bread and wine," these words : who myself adore and would, *if it were necessary or my duty*, teach my people to adore, &c. I added these words, because then and ever since I have only maintained Eucharistical adoration, as a view rightly devotionally resulting from the Church's doctrine of the real objective Presence, but not specifically enjoined in any doctrinal formula.

THE HOLY EUCHARIST.

There are three questions which may be asked in regard to the Holy Eucharist :

1. What is present?
2. Where is it present?
3. How is it present?

To each one of these interrogatories three answers may be given. First, How is it present? The Roman Catholic answers, by Transubstantiation. The Lutheran answers, by Consubstantiation. The Zwinglian answers, Figuratively. The Churchman denies the three, and when pressed to say how Christ is present he answers, 'I cannot tell how; it is a mystery, and I believe and adore.'

The second question is, "What is present?" As to this there are three different views held in the Church :

a. That it is the grace of God's Holy Spirit which is present.
b. That it is a gift which is the same as though it were the body and blood of Christ, and yet is not that body and blood.
c. That it is the body and blood of Christ, though not by Transubstantiation, Consubstantiation, or Figuratively, as the Zwinglians say.

The third question is, "Where is it present?" And here again are three answers:

a. In the heart of the faithful receiver.
b. Before reception, outside of the faithful receiver, but not in connection with the holy elements.
c. After consecration and before reception, in sacramental union with the consecrated elements.

This is my own view. I cannot say how it is present. I deny that it is by Transubstantiation, Consubstantiation, or any other device of human reason. As to what is present, I say it is the body and blood of Christ; and as to where it is present, I assert that it is in sacramental union with the consecrated elements, to be the spiritual food of the faithful.

The view is expressed in a speech made by one of my accusers, the Rev. Dr. Egar, in the General Convention, (p 464 of Debates).

" How gentlemen can stand on this floor and tell us that there is no real Presence in the Sacrament, (I use these words now with a sense of the highest awe, on a most solemn subject, and with sorrow, now that I am obliged to speak in this way, but I cannot permit these statements of doctrine to remain unchallenged,) how can gentlemen deny that there is a real Presence if they have ever learned their Church catechism ? For what does the Church catechism tell us in respect to a sacrament? It tells us that a sacrament consists of two parts—an outward and visible Sign, and an inward and spiritual grace—that is to say, a Sacrament is a whole of which there are two parts, the one visible and the other invisible; that in respect to the Lord's Supper, the visible part is bread and wine; the invisible part is the body and blood of our blessed Lord. Now when you define a Sacrament that is to consist of two parts, one of which is the body and blood, I do not see how you can eliminate from that, the one part, and leave the other part alone. I object then to the doctrinal basis on which this argument has been conducted. I say the gentlemen who have given this definition of a Ritualist which it is designed to put down, are going in the face of the Catechism, and are going in the face of the whole of the doctrine of this Church. That is to say, so far as they have given us a definition of the thing as a tangible thing, they tell you that if you admit that doctrine which the great majority of us here do admit, all these other things follow logically from it."

Let it be noticed, Mr. President, that the "Reverend Deputy from Massachusetts," whom Dr. Egar refers to in his speech and was answering (Dr. Vinton), had said, (p. 392 of the debates) : "That one solitary idea, the presence of Christ in union with the elements of the Sacrament, no matter by what term soever it be designated—corporal, objective, local, hyperphysical—anything that implies the connection, the association or incorporation of the one with the other, was the single idea repudiated by the Reformed Church of England." Dr. Egar, on the other hand, maintained the Sacramental union between the bread and wine and the body and blood of our Lord. In this, too, he is supported by divines almost too many to mention, of the Church of England. I will only give the famous passage of the great Bishop Pearson, (article III. of the Creed, page 238 of Nicholls' edition :

" Vain therefore was that old conceit of Eutyches, who thought the union to be made so in the natures, that the humanity was absorbed and wholly turned into the Divinity, so that by that Transubstantiation the human nature had no longer being. And well did the Ancient Fathers, who opposed this heresy, make use of the Sacramental union between the bread and wine and the body and blood of Christ, and thereby showed that the human nature of Christ is no more really converted into the Divinity, and so ceaseth to be the human nature, than the substance of the bread and wine is really converted into the substance of the body and blood, and thereby ceaseth to be both bread and wine; from whence it is, by the way, observable that the Church in those days understood no such doctrine as that of Transubstantiation."

The note after giving the often quoted passages from Gelasius and Theodoret, which will be given in a quotation hereafter to be made from Bishop Andrewes, concludes with this striking passage : "As therefore all the *metastoicheiosis* (transformation) of *the sacramental elements* maketh them not cease to be of the same nature which before they were, so the human nature of Christ joined to the Divine, loseth not the nature of humanity, but continueth with the Divinity as a substance in itself distinct, and so Christ doth subsist not only *of*, but *in* two natures—as the Council of Chalcedon determined against Eutyches." The same doctrine is taught in the most striking way by Bishop Andrewes in his sermon XVI. of the Nativity, [vol. 1, pp. 282-283 of the Angl. Cath. Lib.:]

"And the gathering or vintage of these two" (Christ, the bread of life, the true vine, and the elements of bread and wine,) "in the blessed Eucharist is, as I may say, a kind of hypostatical union of the sign and the thing signified, so united together as are the two natures of Christ. And even from this sacramental union do the Fathers borrow their resemblance, to illustrate by it the personal union in Christ; I name Theodoret for the Greek, and Gelasius for the Latin Church, that insist upon it both and press it against Eutyches : That even as in the Eucharist, neither part is evacuate or turned into the other, but abide each still in his former nature and substance, no more is either of Christ's natures annulled, or one of them converted into the other, as Eutyches held, but each nature remaineth still full and whole in his own kind. And, backwards, as the two natures in Christ, so the *signum* (sign) and *signatum* (thing signified) in the Sacrament, *e converso*."

The present Bishop of Salisbury, Dr. Moberly, (Bampton Lectures for 1868, p. 171,) sums it all up as follows :

"I will therefore only say that the ancient doctrine of the Church, and as I read it, the unquestionable doctrine of the Church of England is, that the spiritual Presence of the Body and Blood of our Lord in the Holy Communion is objective and real. I do not see how we can consent, as with Hooker and Waterland, to limit authoritatively that presence to the heart of the receiver: for the words of the institution (and these are cases in which we are rigidly and absolutely bound to the exact words of the revelation) the words, I say, of the Lord in the institution seem to forbid such a gloss."

This is the doctrine of the real Presence, I believe ; and which I am sure Dr. Egar, and perhaps all the Professors at Nashotah, hold. I will give also the admirable words of Mr.

Palmer in his Treatise of the Church, vol. ı. part ii, chap. vii, . pp. 526–531.

" Her doctrine concerning the true presence appears to be limited to the following points: "Taking as her immovable foundation the words of Jesus Christ : ' This is My Body; . . This is My Blood of the new covenant;' and ' Whoso eateth My Flesh and drinketh My Blood hath eternal life;' she believes that the Body or Flesh, and the Blood of Jesus Christ, the Creator and Redeemer of the world, both God and Man, united indivisibly in One Person, are verily and indeed given to, taken, eaten, and received by the faithful in the Lord's Supper, under the outward sign or ' form of bread and wine,' which is, on this account, the ' partaking or communion of the Body and Blood of Christ.' She believes that the Eucharist is not the sign of an *absent* body and that those who partake of it receive not merely the figure, or shadow or sign of Christ's Body, but the reality itself. And, as Christ's Divine and Human Natures are inseparably united, so she believes that we receive in the Eucharist, not only the Flesh and Blood of Christ, *but Christ Himself, both God and Man.* Resting on these words, ' The bread which we break is it not the communion of the Body of Christ ?' and again, ' I will not drink henceforth of this fruit of the vine :' she holds that the nature of the bread and wine continues after consecration, and therefore rejects transubstantiation, or ' *the* change of the substance,' which supposes the nature of bread entirely to cease by consecration. As a necessary consequence of the preceding truths, and admonished by Christ Himself, ' It is the spirit that quickeneth, the flesh profiteth nothing : the words that I speak unto you they are spirit and they are life ;' she holds that the Presence (and therefore the eating) of Christ's Body and Blood. though true, is altogether ' heavenly and spiritual,' of a kind which is inexplicable by any carnal or earthly experience or imagination : even as the Sonship of the Eternal Word of God, and His Incarnation, and the procession of the Holy Spirit, are immeasurable by human understandings.

" Believing according to the Scriptures, that Christ ascended in His natural Body into Heaven, and shall only come from thence at the end of the world; she rejects, for this reason, as well as the last, any such real Presence of Christ's Body and Blood as is corporal or organical, that is, according to the known and earthly mode of existence of a body. Resting on the Divine promise, 'Whoso eateth My Flesh and drinketh My Blood hath eternal life,' she regards it as the more pious and probable opinion, that the wicked, those who are totally devoid of true and living faith, do not partake of the Holy Flesh of Christ in the Eucharist, God withdrawing from them so ' divine ' a gift, and not permitting His enemies to partake of it. And hence she holds that such a faith is ' the means by which the body of Christ is received and eaten,' ' a necessary instrument in all these holy ceremonies ;' because it is the essential qualification on our parts, without which that Body is not received.

" Following the example of our Lord Jesus Christ, and of the Apostles,

and supported by their authority, she believes that 'the blessing' or 'consecration' of the bread and wine is not without effect, but that it operates a real
change ; for when the Sacrament is thus perfected, she regards it as so 'divine
a thing,' so 'heavenly a food,' that we must not *presume* to approach it
with unprepared minds, and that sinners, although they only partake of the
bread and wine, partake of them to their own *condemnation*, because they
impiously disregard the Lord's Body, which is truly present in that Sacrament.
Hence it is that the Church believing firmly in the real Presence of the
'precious and Blessed Body and Blood of our Saviour Jesus Christ,' speaks
of the Eucharist as 'high and holy mysteries,' exhorts us to consider the
'dignity of that holy mystery,' that 'heavenly feast,' that 'holy Table,'
'the banquet of that most Heavenly food,' even 'the King of kings'
Table.' "

I will conclude this part of my argument with the words of
a Clergyman in high position in the American Church, the Rev.
Dr. Dix, Rector of Trinity Church, New York. [Manual of
Instruction for Confirmation Classes pp. 53 and 54.]

IV. THE SACRAMENTAL ASPECT.

Three things concur to the completeness of this Holy Mystery in its Sacramental character :

1. *The outward visible sign.*
2. *The inward part and thing signified.*
3. *The benefits conferred thereby.*

These must not be confused ; especially must the second and third be
kept distinct in our thoughts. The inward part is not to be confounded with
the benefits, for they are distinct. The Sacrament is complete in itself when,
by the power of the Holy Ghost, and by the words of Consecration, the Bread
and Wine become the Body and Blood of Christ ; but whether a man receive
benefit or condemnation in partaking, depends on his interior state, the sincerity of his repentance, the strength of his faith, &c.

V. EXPLANATIONS.

1. *The Sign:* called *Sacramentum.* Bread and Wine ; simple elements of daily sustenance. These remain in their proper substance after Consecration, retaining their proper nature. And yet they undergo a mystical
change whereby they become the forms under which Christ is present.

2. *The Thing Signified:* called *Res.* The Body and Blood of Christ ;
His Glorified Humanity, which, after a manner inexplicable and without any
parallel in the range of our knowledge, becomes present after consecration,
not locally or physically, according to the laws of material and carnal bodies,
but supra-locally, hyper-physically, and spiritually, in some way believed on
by the Church but known only to God. The Ancient Catholic Fathers never

sought to explain the Mystery of the Real Presence ; they held it simply and sincerely, loving and adoring.

3. *The Benefits :* called *Virtus.*

These are the results of a faithful and devout reception of the Holy Sacrament :

(*a*) Continuance and maintenance of our union with God through Christ.

(*b*) Assurance of God's favour and goodness towards us (see Post Communion).

(*c*) The forgiveness of sins.

(*d*) The promise of a part in the resurrection of the Just at the last day.

(*e*) The grace, general and special, which is needed for attaining the Divine promises and obtaining the desire of the soul.

EUCHARISTICAL ADORATION.

The doctrine of Eucharistical adoration clearly implied in the last two extracts, is deduced from the doctrine of the Real objective Presence, by the following argument :

1. "The Sacred Humanity of our Lord is inseparable from His Divine Personality, that is from Himself, so that where It is present He is present, the one Christ, both God and man."

2. "The one Christ, both God and man, wheresoever. He is present is adorable."

3. "He is present by virtue of the supernatural presence of the Sacred Humanity in the Blessed Eucharist."

4. Therefore in the Blessed Eucharist. He being present is adorable." (See Defence of the Bishop of Brechin pp. 210 and 211.)

Now I know that this question is one of the most difficult in Theology. Some people who are loud in their denunciations of it do not even know what is meant by it. The ordinary objections to Eucharistic adoration are first, that it is idolatry, or leads thereto. To this I reply.

1. That the worship is not paid to the Holy Elements, though they are to be regarded with reverence.

2. That this worship would not be addressed even to the Body and Blood of Christ, in sacramental union with the Holy Elements, could they be supposed to subsist, (which is impossible, though some seem to hold it), *apart from His Divine Person.*

3. This worship is given and only given to the Divine Person of the Son of God, present in Sacramental union with the Holy Elements. Yet because His person is Divine and Spiritual, not as though He were, or could be confined to that locality.

The second objection is, that it is contrary to the verity of Christ's Human nature, to suppose that it can have a Presence in Sacramental union with the Holy Elements.

To this I reply, that the "corporal Presence of Christ's natural Flesh and Blood" as it is called in the black rubric of the English Prayer Book, can be only at the right Hand of God ; but Christ's glorified Body, which can pass through closed doors, and ascend beyond the farthest stars with a speed infinitely greater than light; this "Spiritual Body" of which St. Paul speaks, may have besides its corporal Presence at the right Hand of God, a *Spiritual* (after the manner of a spirit) Presence in the Holy Sacrament.

And if any one says this may be so, but what proof is there that it is so, I answer in the words of Him who said, "This is my Body, This is my Blood."

The third objection is, That granting the objective Presence of the Body and Blood of Christ in Sacramental union with the Holy Elements, the objective point of all our worship ought to be *Heaven.* 'Our Lord taught us to say "Our Father which art in Heaven." 'The Communion office bids us "Lift up our hearts." 'It may be right to worship Christ by means of the Eucharist, but the worship must be addressed to Heaven.'

To this I reply, that it always seems to me a feeble objection on the part of those who acknowledge an objective Presence. Whether I conceive Heaven opened, and by the eye of faith discern the "Lamb as it had been slain," and myself borne upward there, to be fed by his unfailing love ; or by the same faith, see no longer Altar and Priest and earthly Elements, but behold Christ coming to me and feeding me with Himself; there seems to be no real difference, we worship the same Christ and are fed with the same Gift.

I believe it too, to be contrary to the Holy Scriptures. The Jews were taught to worship God wheresoever He manifested Himself; under human or angelic form; in the burning bush; on Mount Sinai; as the "Captain of the Lord's Host;" in the Pillar of Cloud coming down to the door of the Tabernacle and talking with Moses, which when the people saw, "they worshipped every man in the door of his tent;" in the cloud that filled the Lord's House at the Dedication of the first Temple : and above all in the Shechinah, which either always manifest, or at times revealing its glory, dwelt between the Cherubim. The Theophanies of the old Testament were types of the Incarnation. The Sacrifices of the Jewish church were the shadows of the one Sacrifice of the Cross. If the Holy Eucharist be the Christian Sacrifice, may it not also be the Christian Theophany; and as much demand our worship of the Lord Christ there present, as the Jewish Theophanies did ?

There is a fourth objection, which merely to mention is its refutation. That though the Body and Blood of Christ are really, though Spiritually, present in Sacramental union with the Holy Elements, they are present as slain, and so do not involve the Personal Presence of the Son of God.

But this is bare Nestorianism. When Christ lay in the grave, in the tomb of Joseph of Arimathea, His Body though dead, because It continued to subsist in His Divine Person, was still an object of worship. His Divine Person was no more separate from His Body in the tomb than from His soul in Paradise. Hence they who follow Archdeacon Freeman in this view of his own invention, generally end by becoming disciples of his disciple Canon Trevor, who declares that inasmuch as Christ's Body and Blood as slain exist nowheres now in Heaven or earth, "the Divine thing in the Sacrament is neither a Divine Person nor a Divine substance, but a Divine *quality*, (so to speak) imparted to the bread and wine, whereby they are made the Communion of the Body and Blood of the Cross, and through these of the glorified Body." He adds, and herein I cannot agree with him, "This is no rationalizing interpretation." [Pp. 72 and 73 Sacrifice and Participation of the Holy Eucharist by Canon Trevor.]

I must venture to add another argument, which will serve also to give my views upon the important question of the Eucharistic Sacrifice.

There is nothing clearer in the Holy Scriptures, or more clearly maintained in the Book of Common Prayer, than that Christ "was *once* offered to bear the sins of many ;" that "by *one* offering He hath perfected forever them that are sanctified ;" that there is " no more offering for sin ;" that, in the words of the Prayer Book our Lord made upon the cross " by His one oblation of Himself once offered, a full, perfect and sufficient sacrifice, oblation and satisfaction for the sins of the whole world." On the other hand, while the singleness and sufficiency of the sacrifice of the cross is thus fully declared, the perpetuity of Christ's Priesthood is as carefully revealed. He is constituted a Priest after the " power of an *endless life.*" " He is a Priest *forever*, after the order of Melchisedek." He hath an " intransmissible Priesthood," because "He continueth *ever.*" He is "able to save them to the uttermost that come unto God by Him, seeing He *ever* liveth to make intercession for them." *"This Priesthood of Christ then *being perpetual*, yet employing but a single sacrificial act, must consist in some constant and enduring reference to that one Sacrifice. The Bible tells us what this is. It is the Presence in Heaven, subsisting in the Divine Person of The Son of God, *of the Human Nature of our Lord Jesus.* After His Resurrection His glorified Body still bore the marks of the Passion. St. Thomas was bidden to put his finger into the "print of the nails," and "to thrust his hand into his side." His glorified Body cannot admit of change. It must be now as it was then. Nay, it is prophesied of It : "They shall look on Him whom they have pierced." The angels of God, the redeemed in Paradise, and all living creatures from highest Seraphim to all beneath the sea, cry aloud, "Worthy is the Lamb that was slain." Nay, when the rapt apostle was describing the aweful vision of the thrice Holy Trinity, he beheld, and "lo, in the midst of the throne . . . . . stood a *"Lamb as it had been slain."* Not as a Suppliant, but as a King upon His Priestly throne, the Eternal Son, man as well as God, presents His human nature once slain, now glorified, as our ransom, and by It pleads for our pardon.

No devout Churchman will deny that the Priestly work of Christ in Heaven, finds its counterpart in his Earthly Kingdom

*See Sermons of Archer Butler, 1st series, pp. 144 and 145.

in the various ministrations of His Church, and chiefly in the Holy Eucharist. "It is a memorial before God of the one Sacrifice for sins forever." I use the language of the last Pastoral of the House of Bishops. We "offer these holy gifts unto God" . . . . . . that "we and all Thy whole Church may obtain remission of our sins, and all other benefits of His Passion," says the Prayer of Consecration in the Prayer Book. In short, it is the doing in the Church on earth what our Great High Priest does for us in Heaven. The acts are both His and one.

Since, therefore, the Presence of Christ's Human Nature, once slain, now glorified in Heaven, is the constant reference which is made by the Risen Lord to His one Sacrifice, ought we not to expect a Presence of that same human nature, so far as it can be present, in the Holy Eucharist, in Sacramental union with the Holy Elements. There, locally, here, *sacramentally;* there, after the manner of a Body, here, after the *manner of a Spirit;* yet in both really, truly, certainly, the one and self same Humanity, the same Blessed Person, Sacrifice and Priest, and a call for men on earth, and the Angels in Heaven, and the redeemed in Paradise, to worship and adore the "Lamb as it had been slain."

And if anyone says, This may be so, but what proof is there of it? I answer again in the words of Him who said, "This is my Body; this is my Blood." "Offer this for my own memorial." "He that eateth Me even he shall live by Me."

No doubt there are other objections to Eucharistic adoration and other answers; the question is admittedly a most difficult one. The Church I believe has done wisely in leaving it to the faith and devotion of her children. But if she does not say they *must* hold it, she certainly never says they *must not* hold it; and teaches authoritatively a doctrine from which it is a lawful conclusion. I therefore claim for myself the liberty which I allow to others.

I come now to the proof that she has allowed the doctrine to be held.

Bishop Andrewes is confessedly one of the greatest, if not the greatest Divine of the Church of England. One of the Translators of the Bible, he added to marvelous learning and unequalled eloquence a devotion which has made his Prayers ever since, one of the Church's best possessions. Cardinal Bellarmine, the ablest controversalist of that age upon the Roman side, in Europe, had attacked his Sovereign King James the first. Bishop Andrewes, then Bishop of Ely, was put forth to defend the King. In his reply to Cardinal Bellarmine he stands forth as the champion of his church and King, and though two hundred and fifty years have passed, the Church has never repudiated his noble arguments. To be sure he was carped at in his day also. In a memoir of Bishop Andrewes published by Sir John Harrington, in 1653, it is said that being appointed to that Prebendship in St. Paul's, the holder of which was called the Confessor, " his manner was, especially in Lent time, to walk duly at certain hours in one of the aisles of the Church, that if any came to him for spiritual advice and comfort, (as some did though not many) he might impart it to them. This custom being agreeable to the Scripture and Fathers, not repugning the xxxix articles and required in some sort in the Communion Book, and no less approved by Calvin in his Institutions, yet was quarrelled with as a point of Popery. The like scandal was taken of some, though not given by him, for his reverent speaking of the highest mystery of our faith and heavenly food, the Lord's Supper, which some are so stiff in their knees, or rather in their hearts, that they hold it idolatry to receive it kneeling. But whatsoever such barked at, he ever kept one tenor of life and doctrine, exemplary and unreprovable." [pp. xxxvi and xxxvii of Life of Bishop Andrewes in Angl. Cath. Lib.] And this Judgement of him the voice of the Anglican Communion has ever approved.* I give a quotation from his Reply to Cardinal Bellarmine. The words of the Cardinal are placed in brackets and the replies of the Bishop follow. [Lib. of Angl. Cath Theol. Resp. ad. Bell. pp. 264, 265, 266 and 267.]

[" I will also adduce one writer, who bears the name of S. Cyprian, but who, though not the very celebrated martyr Cyprian, is yet of very ancient and weighty authority . . . " The bread being changed, not in form, but in nature, by the omnipotence of the word, became flesh" . . . . He says, that the nature, that is, the substance, is changed ; and that the form, that is, the accidents, are not changed."] [Bell. Apol. pro Resp. p. 107. Op. tom. vii. col. 764, C. D.]

*For a reply to the Churchman of Feb. 7th, impugning Bishop Andrewes. See appendix iii.

" Now that weighty author (who bears the name of Cyprian and yet is not Cyprian) says that the bread is changed in nature, not in form; and this is not denied by us either. But we nevertheless deprecate the interpretation of the Cardinal, "nature, that is, substance; and form, that is, accidents." For what that author says is, that by the addition of the omnipotence of the word, the nature is changed, so that what was before a mere element, becomes now a Divine Sacrament, while nevertheless the previously existing substance still remains. This is shown by the words which immediately follow; they being both part of the same passage, and always by you fraudulently left out, namely, " And just as in the person of Christ the humanity was seen and the divinity was hidden; so the Divine essence infused itself into the visible Sacrament;" meaning doubtless that the union between the visible Sacrament, and the invisible inward part of the Sacrament is the same as that which exists between the humanity and the Divinity of Christ; where, unless you mean to be a Eutychian, the humanity is not transubstantiated into the divinity. But, that you may know that the word "nature" is not to be understood as meaning "substance" in that passage where Peter says, "that we are made partakers of the divine nature," that same author (and in the same passage too) denies that this kind of unity is equivalent to a consubstantiality with Christ. Substance, therefore the Cardinal finds nowhere asserted, while we find it denied. Theodoret says, "For the symbols remain in their former substance." Moreover Gelasius, Pontifex and Chief Pastor, to whose words all Papists must listen, says that the symbols "by the operation of the Holy Spirit pass over into the divine substance (wherefore I marvel that this writer is omitted by the Cardinal), and yet that the substance or nature of the bread and wine does not cease to exist." Moreover, in order more clearly to indicate to us his meaning, he adds these words " Just as Christ (says he), being One, consists of natures separately remaining." Both, Gelasius as well as Theodoret, contradict Eutyches. Hence it is clearly manifest that the transmutation which takes place in the Sacrament, is not one of substance. I quote also the following words of Augustine : " This is what we assert, and what we claim in every manner to prove, namely that the Sacrafice of the Eucharist consists of two things, the visible species of the elements, and the invisible flesh and blood of Christ (the Sacrament and the inward part of the Sacrament); just as the person of Christ consists and is composed of God and Man, since Christ Himself is very God and very Man. Because everything contains in itself the nature and verity of those things of which it is composed. Moreover the Sacrament of the Church is composed of two things, the Sacrament and the inward part of the Sacrament, that is, the body of Christ."

[He classes as a novel and recent dogma the Adoration of the Sacrament of the Eucharist, that is, the Adoration of the Lord Christ, wonderfully but truly present in the Sacrament.] [Bell. Apol. pro Resp. p. 107. Op. tom. vii. col. 764 D.]

In the phrase " Adoration of the Sacrament " he disgracefully stumbles upon the very threshold, "of the Sacrament, he says, that is, of the Lord Christ wonderfully but truly present in the Sacrament." But away with it! Who would grant him this? "Of the Sacrament, *that is*, of Christ in the Sacrament?" [*i. e.* that the Sacrament and Christ in the Sacrament are the same.] "Nay, rather *Christ Himself, the inward part of the Sacrament* [res Sacramenti.] *in and with the Sacrament,* [Sacramentum] *apart from and without the Sacrament, wherever He is, is to be adored.* Now the King maintained that Christ truly present in the Eucharist, was also truly to be adored; that is to say, the inward part of the Sacrament; but not the Sacrament, that is to say, the earthly part, according to Irenaeus; the visible part, according to Augustine."

[S. Ambrose says . . . . "We adore the flesh of Christ in the mysteries" . . . S. Gregory, Nazian. . . . commending the piety of Gorgoria, thus writes . . . "Beseeching Him who is worshipped upon the altar". . . Now what that which is worshipped upon the altar, S. Optatus of Mileum shows, who in his third book against Parmenianus calls the altar the resting place of the Body and Blood of Christ. Augustine says . . . No one eats unless he has first adored." [Bell. 'Apol. pro Resp. pp 107 and 108, Op. tom. vii. col. 765. A. B.]

But we indeed also, with Ambrose, adore the flesh of Christ in the mysteries, and not, "*that*" but "*Him*" who is worshipped upon the altar. For the Cardinal improperly asks "What is worshipped there" when he should have asked "Who" since he of Nazianzum says "Him" not "that." And neither do we, with Augustine, eat the flesh without first adoring. And yet we by no means adore the Sacrament. [Sacramentum.]

I give next the following quotations from Herbert Thorndike's "Laws of the Church." Born in 1598, he was 28 years of age when Bishop Andrewes died. As a student at Cambridge University he belonged to the Diocese of Ely, while Bishop Andrewes was its Bishop, and it was in the first year of his studentship there, that Bishop Andrewes attended King James in a visit to the great University. It was during the great Rebellion that he was chosen for his knowledge of Syriac, to assist in one of the noblest enterprises of English theological scholarship, the publication of Walton's Polyglot. It was during the same period that he wrote the remarkable book from which the following extract is taken. But I need say no more about him, than that Bishop Bull calls him the "Blessed :"

"But I suppose, further, that the Body and Blood of Christ is not adored, nor to be adored by Christians, neither for Itself, nor for any endowment residing in It, which It may have received by being personally united with the Godhead of Christ; *but only in consideration of the said Godhead, to which It*

remains inseparably united, wheresoever It becomes. For by that means, whosoever proposeth not to himself the consideration of the Body and Blood of
Christ, as It is of Itself and in Itself a mere creature (which he, that doth not
on purpose, cannot do) cannot but consider It, as he believes It to be, being a
Christian; and considering It as It is, *honour It as It is inseparably united to
the Godhead,* in which and by which It subsisteth; in which, therefore, that
honour resteth, and to which it tendeth. So the Godhead of Christ is a thing
that is honoured, and the reason why it is honoured, both: the Body and
Blood of Christ, though It be necessarily honoured, because necessarily united
to that which is honoured; yet is It only the thing that is honoured and not the
reason why It is honoured, speaking of the honour proper to God alone."
[Vol. iv. p. 754. Angl. Cath. Lib.]

" And is not the presence thereof in the Sacrament of the Eucharist a just
occasion, presently to express by the bodily act of adoration that inward honour
which we always carry towards our Lord Christ as God?" [P. 754.] . . . .

"Here then you see I am utterly disobliged to dispute, whether or no in
the ancient Church Christians were exhorted and encouraged to, and really
did, worship our Lord Christ in the Sacrament of the Eucharist. For having
concluded my intent, that it had not been idolatry had it been done, I might
leave the consequence of it to debate. But not to balk the freedom which hath
carried me to publish all this, I do believe that it was so practised and done in
the ancient Church, which I maintain from the beginning to have been the
true Church of Christ, obliging all to conform to it in all things within the
power of it. I know the consequence to be this, that there is no good cause
why it should not be done at present, but that cause which justifies the reform-
ing of some part of the Church without the whole; which, if it were taken
away, that it might be done again, and ought not to be of itself alone any
cause of distance."

" For I do acknowledge the testimonies that are produced out of S.
Ambrose, *De Spiritu Sancto,* iii. 12; S. Augustine, *in Psalm,* xcviii., and
Epist. cxx. cap. xxvii.; S. Chrysostom, *Homil,* xxiv, *in* 1 *ad Corinth* ;
Theodoret, *Dial,* ii.; S. Gregory Nazianzen, *Orat, in S. Gorgoniam ;* S. Jer-
ome, *Epist. ad Theophilum Episc. Alexandriae ;* Origen, *In diversa loca
Evang.,* *Hom.* v., where he teacheth to say at the receiving the Sacrament,
' Lord, I am not worthy that Thou shouldst come under my roof,' which to say
is to do that which I conclude. Nor do I need more to conclude it." ·

"And what reason can I have not to conclude it? Have I supposed the
elements, which are God's creatures, in which the sacrament is celebrated, to
be abolished; or anything else, concerning the Flesh and Blood of Christ,
or the presence thereof in the Eucharist, in giving a reason why the Church
may do it, which the Church did not believe? If I have, I disclaim it as soon
as it may appear to me for such. Nay, I do expressly warn all opinions,
that they imagine not to themselves the Eucharist so mere and simple a sign
of the thing signified, that the celebration thereof should not be a competent

occasion *for the executing of that worship, which is always due to our Lord Christ incarnate.*

"I confess it is not necessarily the same thing to worship Christ in the Sacrament of the Eucharist, as to worship the Sacrament of the Eucharist, yet in that sense which reason of itself justifieth, it is. For the Sacrament of the Eucharist, by reason of the nature thereof, is neither the visible kind, nor the invisible grace, of Christ's Body and Blood, but the union of both by virtue of the premises; in regard whereof the one going along with the other, what-soever be the distance of their nature, both concur to that, which we call the Sacrament of the Eucharist, by the work of God, to which He is morally en-gaged by the promise which the institution thereof containeth. If this be rightly understood, to worship the Sacrament of the Eucharist is to worship Christ in the Sacrament of the Eucharist."—(pp. 755-757, vol. iv, Angl. Cath. Lib.)

My next quotation is taken from the "Considerationes Mod-estæ" of Bishop William Forbes of Edinburgh, who died in 1634. This work was transcribed by the great Bishop Cosin :

" As regards the adoration of this Sacrament, since " he who worthily receives the sacred symbols, truly and really receives into himself the Body and Blood of Christ, corporeally, yet in a certain spiritual, miraculous, and imperceptible manner, everyone who worthily communicates can and ought to adore the Body of Christ which he receives; not because it is hid corporeally in the bread, or under the bread, or under the species and accidents of bread : but because, when the sacramental bread is worthily received, then along with the bread, the real Body of Christ, which is really present in that communion, is also received," as the Archbishop of Spalatro says. "We adore the Flesh of Christ in the mysteries;' says S. Ambrose; S. Gregory Nazianzen, "Calling upon Him who is worshipped upon the altar," S. Augustine—"No one eateth that Flesh (viz.; that of Christ,) till he have first adored." See S. Chrysostom in several parts of his writings. The rest of the ancients agree.

" Enormous is the error of the more rigid Protestants who deny that Christ is to be adored in the Eucharist, save with an internal and mental adoration, but not with any outward rite of worship, as by kneeling, or some other similar position of the body. They with few exceptions hold wrong views concerning the presence of Christ the Lord in the Sacrament, who is present in a wonderful but true manner." [Lib. of Ang. Cath. Theol., vol ii, p. 545]

"As regards the first assertion of Bellarmine about venerating the sym-bols with a kind of lesser reverence, we admit it; but what he says of the adoration of *latria*, that though *per se* and properly it be due and exhibited to Christ, yet it belongs also to the symbols, in so far as they are apprehended as one, in a certain respect with Christ Himself Whom they contain, and to Whom they are a covering and concealment, like garments; is false and repugnant to the opinion of very many others. For these species do not belong to the person of Christ nor do they make one with It. Whence he himself a little while after doubtingly says : "Whatever there may be said of the expressions used, the state of the question simply is, whether *Christ in the Eucharist* is to be adored with the worship of *latria*." But this the *more sound Protestants do not doubt ;* "for in the reception of the Eucharist," to use the words of the Archbishop of Spalatro, "Christ is to be adored with true *latria*, since His living and glorious Body is present to the worthy receiver by a certain inexplicable miracle; and this adoration is due and is paid, not to the bread, not to the wine, not to the participation, not to the eating, not to the sign, but immediately to Christ's Body itself, exhibited through the partaking of the Eucharist." [page 551.]

I give these extracts, Mr. President, not as though they were all which could be given, but as sufficient to show that the doctrine of Eucharistical adoration has been allowed in the Church of England. Is any one here prepared to say that such men as Andrewes, Bishop Forbes of Edinburgh, and Thorndike, whose lives covered almost the whole period from the Reformation to the fatal day, when the accession of William and Mary, drove out the piety and holiness of Sancroft and Ken ; that in our own time the saintly Bishop Hamilton of Salisbury, and John Keble, the author of the Christian Year, who are at rest with God ; and the Bishop of Brechin, Dr. Pusey, and Canon Liddon, who still fight the good fight, are disloyal to the Church of their Baptism.

But surely all this is scarcely necessary, at least so far as my six accusers are concerned, when I am able to quote in my behalf even Dr. Adams himself. Immediately after my last speech in the General Convention of 1871, Dr. Adams said: [p. 513 of Debates.]

"Now I wish to say that upon this matter of the Holy Eucharist, the question is the most dubious and the most debated matter in Europe for a thousand years. The doctrine which Dr. De Koven holds, I believe, is the same as that of Dr. Pusey. It is identical, more or less, with the old doctrine of consubstantiation. I do not wish the clergy and laity in this House to get scared and talk about a difficult question, and get into an excitement and imagine that Dr. De Koven is coming here and speaking heresy. Dr. De Koven—

The President : You will please speak of your colleague as your colleague, and not mention his name.

Dr. Adams : I beg pardon. My colleague is *not a heretic in any shape or form.* He holds a doctrine *which is tolerated* in the Church, as every other doctrine, except Zwinglianism, is" etc.

It must be noted that Dr. Adams does not venture to accuse me of holding Consubstantiation. He says it is identical, *"more or less,"* with that doctrine. He, however, asserts that it is a doctrine to be tolerated.

I quote the testimony of Dr. Adams knowing that it was an unwilling testimony. He follows up this admission by charging me with being "a shrewd and able party leader." (Page 513 of Debates.) He knew well that whatever force there was in my argument before the Convention, was due to its sincerity.—If the confidence of the Church could be shaken in this, all else would be of no avail. This too has been the motive of the attacks of the *Church Journal,* viz., the endeavour to show what cannot be proved by any action of my life, that I am not one contending for great truths, but the leader of a party. I quote the words, however, because, though like Balaam Dr. Adams intended to harm, like Balaam he was constrained to bless.

Let me add for myself, that I believe our Church tolerates certain views of the Eucharist, which may fall short of the doctrine of the Real objective Presence, and which are not Zwinglian. I do not say this, however, *in the interests of Latitudinarianism.* As Sir Robert Phillimore expresses it in his "Judgement :" "The objective, actual and Real Presence, or the spiritual Real Presence, a Presence external to the act of the communicant, appears to me to be the doctrine which the Formularies of our Church, duly considered and construed so as to be harmonious, intended to maintain." But while she distinctly asserts this, and maintains it against Transubstantiation on the one side, and Zwinglianism on the other, and is thus at one with the Catholic Church, for twelve hundred years ; with that broad hearted spirit, which distinguishes her from a sect, she tolerates some feebler views. She does so, however, because so far as they go they are true—imperfect views, it may be, but still the truth of God.

E. g. The Holy Eucharist is a commemoration,—*but not a mere commemoration.*

The Holy Eucharist is made what it is by the Presence of God's Holy Spirit ; and brings in it His Blessed grace,—*but it has in it also a specific gift.*

The Holy Eucharist has in it virtually the Body and Blood of Christ,—because it has them *really*.

The faithful recipient is indeed a partaker of Christ. "Christ dwells in him, and he in Christ,"—*because Christ is present before reception to give Himself.*

One thing more I must say in the interests of the Church at large. There seems to be a notion prevailing that such a doctrine as that of Eucharistical adoration may be tolerated in a Presbyter, but is somehow a proper reason for refusing to such a person preferment or office, for which in other respects he may be fitted.

But such an idea will not bear a moments examination. Has our Church one set of doctrines she allows to Deacons, another to Presbyters, and another to Bishops? May one like myself, who has had a thousand or more of boys and young men under his charge, some thirty of whom are now either in the Holy ministry or preparing for it, and nearly four hundred of whom have been prepared by him for confirmation and first communion, be allowed to maintain doctrines some one else may not? If it be so, will some one of these, my accusers, tell us just what the doctrine of the Eucharist is, which will fit a man for preferment? Let us know what Shibboleth the ambitious mouth must pronounce. Nay, I will venture to make to them a profitable suggestion. There are varying views and tolerated opinions on other subjects besides the Eucharist. Let them compile a Treatise. Let them teach those who wish to learn, the exact doctrinal steps which lead safely on. To be sure from time to time revised editions will need to be published, as the theological barometer goes up or down. The same rule would scarce admit Bishop Hobart and Bishop Meade ; Bishop Alonzo Potter and Bishop De Lancey ; Bishop McIlvaine and Bishop Doane of New Jersey. Nay, for a book so important, I am tempted even to give suggestions for the binding. Bind it not, O, my friends, in russia, lest it seem to be too friendly to the Greek Church. As it is to be a book for the use of shepherds, beware of the sad suggestion of sheep skin. Let it be sent forth in *boards;* then will it be purchased by that party which our Fathers knew not, which is neither high, nor low, nor broad, but pre-eminently what may be called *hard* Church. And when the work is done, if it be accepted, Mr. President, farewell to the brave old days and the brave old men, out of whose differences often came the higher truth ; farewell to high-toned earnestness and straight forward independence, and to the grand heritage of toleration of our Mother Church.

Now, Mr. President, I have, as fully as the circumstances admit of, stated the doctrine of the Eucharist which I hold. So far as this document has not misrepresented it, I have no fault to find. I come now to its

UTTER UNFAIRNESS,

as found in the following paragraph.

"Still it may be argued, on behalf of Dr. DeKoven and the ritualists, that this is merely a speculative opinion, especially as the Dr. explicitly disavows a belief in Transubstantiation. But unfortunately the practical results of this belief, are identical with the practical results of Transubstantiation, and the difference is merely speculative and nugatory as between his belief and that of the church of Rome. For the acts of adoration addressed to the Presence in the Elements on the Altar, are precisely those addressed by the members of the Church of Rome to the Host, and none other. This localization of the Presence, implies an arrangement of the service, with lights, vestments, prostrations, non-communicant adorations, a reserved Sacrament, processions of Corpus Christi, and all other incidents with which the attendants on Roman Catholic worship are familiar, and which are foreign to our own "use." It implies an offering of Christ by the Priest for the living and the dead—it implies in every respect, what the ritualists call it, the Mass, and not the Holy Communion." [Principles, not Men.]

At first sight, my brethren, you will scarcely understand the full force of this paragraph. Let me review my argument :

1. I have shown that the great divines of the Church of England, in exact accordance with the Prayer Book, teach the doctrine of the real objective Presence.

2. That it is a logical and devotional result of that doctrine that Christ our Lord, present in Sacramental union with the Holy Elements, is to be adored.

3. That the Church, however, has never commanded Eucharistical adoration in any specific doctrinal formula, or by any other ritual expression than the command to kneel when her children receive.

4. Believing, in Eucharistical adoration, it is therefore necessary, and my duty to teach it, in the same measure and to the
same degree as the Church has permitted it to be taught.

But there are two methods of teaching, one by word of
mouth, another by ritual. I suppose many of the objections
against believing and teaching Eucharistical adoration, which have
been of late in the mouths of men, *have been intended against
the latter*. No one could forbid a man to believe or to teach that
Christ in the Eucharist is to be adored with *acts of mental adoration*.
To show this clearly, one has only to state the fact that the Judicial
Committee of the Privy Conncil gave it as one reason for the acquittal of Mr. Bennett from the charge of unlawful adoration, that
"Some of their Lordships have doubted whether the word 'adore,'
though it seems to point rather to acts of worship, such as are
forbidden by the 28th Article, may not be construed to refer to
mental adoration, or prayers addressed to Christ present spiritually in the Sacrament, which *does not necessarily imply any adoration of the consecrated elements or of any corporal or natural pres
ence therein.*" [Judgement of Judicial Committee in the case of
Shepard vs. Bennett, p 302 of Mr. Stephen's Argument, &c.]

I beg, Mr. President, your especial attention to this grave distinction, well known to all who have thought upon the subject,
between acts of mental adoration, the out-pouring of the heart,
and acts of *ritual adoration*, which might be supposed to mean
and teach much more than the adoration of Christ present in
Sacramental Union with the Holy Elements.

It might be "necessary and my duty" to do and teach the former, it might *not* "be necessary or my duty" to do and teach
the latter. But in order to condemn me it was necessary to show
that I practised not simply mental adoration but ritual adoration :
and hence this paragraph.

Fully to investigate the accusation and to explain its grievous
wrong, allow me to arrange these various sorts of ritual in three
divisions.

1. " Lights and vestments."
2. " Incense and Prostrations."
3. " A reserved Sacrament" (for purposes of worship.)
" Processions of Corpus Christi." " All other incidents with

which the attendants upon Roman Catholic worship are familiar;" including I suppose the Benediction of the Blessed Sacrament. The forty hours Exposition &c., &c.

I classify them in this way to show the skill with which the paragraph is framed. Those under the third class alone are distinctly Roman. The Lutherans who certainly are Protestant enough have both lights and vestments. The Greek Church and the Communions who have separated from it, the Nestorian and Jacobite Churches, have Lights, Vestments, Incense and Prostrations. The Lutheran church holds the doctrine known as Consubstantiation. The Greek Church holds the Catholic faith of all ages as to the Eucharist. Accused as she is sometimes of holding Transubstantiation, it can only be said of her, that she uses the term "*metousiosis*," but denies that it is to be taken to define the manner in which the bread and wine are changed into the Body and Blood of our Lord. [Neale's Int. to Hist. of the Holy E. Ch. p. 1173 note.] One would reasonably argue therefore that these four things were not *necessarily* the ritual of Transubstantiation. There is proof, however, on the matter which to a member of the Anglican Communion is absolutely unanswerable.

The doctrine of Transubstantiation was imposed upon the Western Church by the fourth Lateran council A. D. 1215. The great Anglican Theologians prove most conclusively that this doctrine was a new one and cannot be proved by Scripture or the Fathers. Lights, Incense, and Vestments date back at least to the 5th century and probably to a far earlier period. I take the latest date. The Jacobite and Nestorian Communions separated from the Eastern Church in that century, and probably have not since changed their usages. Both the orthodox Communions and these heretical bodies had them then, and retain them still. The use of them is seven hundred years and more older than Transubstantiation. Now mark the argument. If they be *necessarily* the ritual of Transubstantiation, all the arguments of our Theologians go for nothing, and the doctrine instead of being a corruption of the middle ages is at least as old as the age of the undisputed General Councils. So do these gentlemen in their eager zeal play into the hands of Rome.

Holding this view, namely, that they are not *necessarily* the ritual of Transubstantiation, but simply the ritual of the Real Presence, I have been the Pastor of a College Chapel. In such a service large liberties have always been allowed. The Rev. Dr. Kemper might have taken in the savour of incense, and I know not what besides, in his boyhood at Dr. Muhlenberg's famous School at College Point. Nay the chapel of Racine College has never been consecrated. It has no legal position as a church. It is nothing more than a private room. Subject always to the authority of the Trustees, so far as ecclesiastical authority was concerned, I might have had the "use of Sarum" had I desired to do so.

Now, mark me, Mr. President, when I say that with all this, the ritual at Racine does *not materially differ*, as these gentlemen well know, *from that which prevails at Nashotah Chapel*, which is a Parish church; and is not so advanced in its character as the ritual in Trinity Church New York, and its Chapels.

The Rev. Mr. Wilkinson from some remark of mine has insinuated to this Body that this moderation has been due to policy or timidity. Let me state to what principles of action it has been due.

1. While I hold that every rubric of the Prayer Book must be obeyed, I do not believe the Prayer Book to be a Book of full ritual directions.

2. I do not believe that by adding to the Prayer Book some vague notion of usage, the law of the Church on the subject of ritual is to be found.

3. I do not think that the Church has a distinct and clear law of ritual.

4. I hope the day may come when we can approach the question of what that law must be, in a spirit of charity; and when we do, I hope we shall find room for both lofty ceremonial, and for simple services.

5. Meanwhile individual action, and sometimes irregular action, has preceded, as it always does, corporate action.

I myself in adopting any ornament or ceremony have been governed by five distinct practical ideas.

1. That it should not contradict any doctrine of the Church.

2. That it should have common sense in its favour.

3. That it should not provoke vehement controversy among those for whose benefit it was intended.

4. That it should not be unreal, but for the good of souls.

5. That it should not be against the command of the Bishop.

Inasmuch therefore as my principles do not. necessarily involve any one of the ceremonies which are distinctly and exclusively Roman, inasmuch as with the exception of Lights on the altar at early celebrations, and on some great festivals at a late one, I have never practiced any one of the three classes of ceremonies enumerated ; I charge my Brethren with grave misrepresentation in this paragraph.*

I come now Mr. President to the subject of

CONFESSION.

Here, too, I must make a distinction. I must state what I hold, and what I do not hold; what I do, and what I do not practice. I suppose that nobody doubts that Confession of some sort is allowed in the Church of England. Enforced upon every communicant before the Reformation, after the year 1215 ; the first Prayer Book of Edward the VI. had the following in the exhortation to the Holy Communion, distinctly showing both what the Church of England meant to forbid, and what it meant to allow :

" If there be any of you whose conscience is troubled and grieved in anything, lacking comfort or counsel, let him come to me or to some other discreet and learned priest, taught in the law of God, and confess and open his sin and grief secretly, that he may receive such ghostly counsel, advice and comfort, that his conscience may be relieved, and that of us, (as of the ministers of God and of the Church) he may receive comfort and absolution, to the satisfaction of his mind, and avoiding all scruple and doubtfulness: requiring such as shall be satisfied with a general confession not to be offended with them that so use to their further satisfying the auricular and secret confession · to the Priest; nor those also which think needful or convenient, for the quietness of their own consciences, particularly to open their sins to the priest, to

*A white linen Alb and Chasuble are used at the celebration of the Lord's Supper in the Chapel of Racine College.

be offended with them that are satisfied with their humble confession to God, and the general confession to the Church; but in all things to follow and keep the rule of charity, and every man to be satisfied with his own conscience, not judging other men's consciences; whereas he has no warrant of God's word to the same."

After some alteration in 1552, this part of the Communion exhortation received in 1661 the form which it has now in the English Prayer Book, viz.:

"And because it is requisite that no man should come to the Holy Communion but with a full trust in God's mercy and with a quiet conscience; therefore if there be any of you, who by this means cannot quiet his own conscience herein, but requireth further comfort or counsel, let him come to me or to some other discreet and learned minister of God's word, and open his grief; that by the ministry of God's holy word he may receive the benefit of absolution, together with ghostly counsel and advice, to the quieting of his conscience, and avoiding of all scruple and doubtfulness."

The exhortation in our own Prayer Book is as follows:

" And because it is requisite that no man should come to the Holy Communion but with a full trust in God's mercy, and with a quiet conscience; therefore, if there be any of you, who by this means cannot quiet his own conscience herein, but requireth further comfort or counsel, let him come to me or to some other minister of God's word, and open his grief; that he may receive such godly counsel and advice, as may tend to the quieting of his conscience and the removing of all scruple and doubtfulness."

I pass over every other passage in the English Prayer Book and in our own that may bear upon the subject. I do not here take up the question of Absolution,* public or private, because the Document does not speak of it, and I assert, that no one can deny that these exhortations literally and historically, clearly show, that Confessions in certain states of mind, of which the communicant is to be the sole judge, are approved of, in the church of England and our own. Nor am I able to accept what seems to me to be an illogical deduction, that because the Church advises it in certain cases, she therefore necessarily forbids it in all others. Nor have these been mere exhortations which have influenced no one. From the Reformation to the present day, many of the noblest and most devout of the children of the Church of England, have found peace and forgiveness in the use of this blessed privilege.

*See Appendix iv.

Visitation articles of such Bishops as Overall, (who wrote the part of the Church catechism about the Sacraments), in 1619, Andrewes, (whose custom has been previously mentioned), in 1625, Cosin, as Archdeacon of York, in 1627, Montague, in 1687, enquire whether the minister exhorts people to come to ghostly counsel and comfort, and the benefit of absolution, and whether the minister reveals the things confessed.

The 113th Canon, of 1603, passed half a century after the Reformation, one of that very set of canons, a portion of which many in the last General Convention desired to reenact, and to which I was opposed, has this clause in it : "Provided always that if any man confess his secret and hidden sins to the minister, for the unburdening of his conscience and to receive spiritual consolation and ease of mind from him," . . . . . . the clergyman is not to reveal what is confessed (except crimes, the concealment of which would endanger his own life), on pain of irregularity.

In the Convocation of 1640, though the acts of the Convocation were not confirmed by Royal authority; it was made one of the enquiries which were to be made in all visitations, whether revelations had been made of things confessed.' Nay, in that very Irish Church in which Dr. Adams was born and bred, a canon (canon xix of the Church of Ireland,) was drawn up in the primacy of Archbishop Ussher, by the great Bramhall, and passed in 1634, and afterwards reenacted in 1701 ; which provided that the minister of the Parish should give warning by the tolling of a bell, or otherwise, "to the intent that if any have any scruple of conscience or desire the special ministry of reconciliation, he may afford it to those who need it ;" and the people are to be exhorted to self examination that they may resort unto God's ministers not only for advice and counsel, but also for "the benefit of absolution, likewise, for the quieting of their consciences, by the power of the keys which Christ has committed to His ministers for that purpose." I believe that during the last two or three years, while the Irish Church has been standing on the very verge of the denial of the truth, (which may God avert !) this canon has been repealed ; but for more than two hundred years after it was enacted, it was the law of the Irish Church.

The testimonies of Bishops and Doctors in the Church of England are almost without number. They include the noblest names and the fairest lives our mother Church and mother land have known.

Dr. Donne, who died in 1631 and was Dean of St. Pauls in King James I. reign says, in one of his sermons; (vol. v. p. 434.)

"For Confession, we require public confession in the Congregation: and in time of sickness upon the death bed, we enjoin private and particular Confession, if the conscience be oppressed; and if any man do think that that which is necessary for him upon his death bed, is necessary every time he comes to the Communion, and so come to such a Confession, if anything lie upon him, as often as he comes to the Communion we blame not, we dissuade not, we discounsel not, that tenderness of conscience and that safe proceeding in the soul."

Bishop Cosin who was one of those engaged in the last revision of the English Prayer book, and whose Book of devotions was, when I was at Nashotah as a Tutor, the authorized book of devotions there, gives it as one of the Precepts of the Church; [p. 121 of vol. ii. of works in Angl. Cath. Lib.]

"And for better preparation thereunto, (the Holy Communion) as occasion is, to disburthen and quiet our consciences of those sins that may grieve us, or scruples that may trouble us, to a learned and discreet Priest, and from him to receive advice and the benefit of absolution."

Similar quotations might be given from such men as Hammond and Heylin, the great Ussher, holy George Herbert, and Bishop Hall, from the judicious Hooker and Jeremy Taylor, from Sparrow, Pearson and Patrick. Most churchmen have no conception of the abundance of authorities, of the clearness of the statements and of the undoubted truth of the fact, that the great divines of the church, have maintained the rights of the children of the church to confess their sins to Almighty God in the presence of a Priest, as need might require. I will conclude the extracts with the words of Archbishop Wake, who died in 1737.

"The Church of England refuses no sort of confession either public or private, which may be any way necessary to the quieting of mens' consciences or to exercising that power of binding and loosing which our Saviour Christ has left to His church. We have our penitential canons for public offences, we exhort men if they have any the least doubt or scruple, nay sometimes though they have none, but especially before the Holy Sacrament, to confess their sins. We propose to them the benefit not only of ghostly advice how to manage their repentance, but the great comfort of absolution too as soon as they shall have completed it." [Exposition of Doctrine of the Church of England pp. 42 and 43.]

What these great Divines taught they also practiced. Archbishop Laud records in his Diary that he had been appointed Confessor to the Duke of Buckingham. Bishop Sanderson who died in 1663, the day before his death received absolution from Mr. Pullin his chaplain, "pulling off his cap that Mr. Pullin might lay his hand upon his bare head." After this desire of his was satisfied, his body seemed to be more at ease and his mind more cheerful, and he said, "Lord forsake me not now my strength faileth me; but continue thy mercy and let my mouth be filled with thy praise." [Walton's Life of Sanderson p. 428.] The saintly Bishop Wilson who wrote the "Sacra Privata," thanked God that his wife had confessed, and received absolution in her last illness (1705). Bishop Ken pronounced an absolution little deserved and heeded over the dying Charles II. (see Macaulay's Hist.); and to sum up all I give the account which Isaac Walton the typical English layman gives, of the practice in life and death, of the great Hooker, the typical English Divine. [Lives pp. 248 and 249]. Let it be noted that the Dr. Saravia spoken of, was a clergyman who had left Holland because of his belief in Episcopacy, and had received preferment in the Church of England, and was afterwards one of the Translators of the English Bible.

"About one day before his death, Dr. Saravia, who knew the very secrets of his soul—*for they were supposed to be Confessors to each other*—came to him and, after a conference of the benefit, the necessity, and safety of the Church's absolution, it was resolved the Doctor should give him both that and the Sacrament the following day. To which end the Doctor came and after a short retirement and privacy they two returned to the company; and then the Doctor gave him and some of those friends that were with him, the blessed Sacrament of the Body and Blood of our Jesus. Which being performed the Doctor thought he saw a reverend gaiety and joy in his face . . . . the day following he found him deep in contemplation and not inclinable to discourse; which gave the Doctor occasion to require his present thoughts. To which he replied "That he was meditating the number and nature of angels, and their blessed obedience and order, without which, peace could not be in Heaven; and oh! that it might be so on earth !"

I may venture perhaps to add a proof which is not exactly

theological. The novelist Thackeray, who certainly wrote in no theological interest, but who was too great a writer, not to be true to history; in his novel of Henry Esmond, describing the times of Queen Anne, makes Lady Esmond go to confession, when troubled in conscience, to the famous Dr. Atterbury, and receive absolution from him.

All this does not need to be proved to any theologian. The six Presbyters are as well aware of it as I am. But the laity whom they have addressed are not. They have been scared with a word. This has been the first injustice. A graver wrong is to be found in the three following passages of "Principles not Men."

1. That I teach "Auricular confession as having a sacramental character, and therefore useful for all Christians as an *ordinary means of the forgiveness of sins..*"

2. That "The members of the Church are to be persuaded, as an ordinary and frequent thing, to come to auricular confession and to put their consciences *iu 'holy obedience' under the Priest's 'direction.'*"

3. "If Dr. De Koven is made Bishop of Wisconsin, the necessary tendency of his principles and associations will be, to require an arrangement of the Episcopal Cathedral, identical with that of Bishop Henni's Cathedral; the Altar must be decorated with lights; the priest must be dressed in vestments, the people must prostrate themselves at the elevation of the Host, the confessional boxes must line the walls, the people will not know whether they are in one or the other," etc.

If the last paragraph be so overstrained that it naturally produces laughter, none the less do the three passages make a charge against me of utter disloyalty and unfaithfulness to the Church. I have quoted the views and practices of a long line of divines of the Church of England. Any controversialist by examining the writings of some of them, notably of Hooker, Ussher and Jeremy Taylor, can bring forward the strongest language against Confession. And why? Because the Church of England has a distinct doctrine on the subject of confession, which clearly distinguishes it from that of Rome. When they advocate confession they mean the confession their own Church permits, approves and advises. When they speak against confession, they mean the system which the Reformation reformed.

There are five chief points in which the Church of England differs from that of Rome.

DIFFERENCES BETWEEN ROME AND ENGLAND ON CONFESSION.

1. Rome believes that imperfect sorrow or attrition becomes contrition or perfect sorrow by means of Confession.

The Church of England denies this as a necessary consequence ; and so do I.

2. Rome teaches that there are two kinds of punishment due to sin, eternal and temporal. It subdivides the latter into the punishments to be borne in this life, and those in purgatory. Absolutions remit the former, the latter are taken away by Penances. Hence sprang up the necessity of "numbering sins," and the whole theory of indulgences.

The Church of England denies this and so do I, regarding with her, acts of penance as useful and desirable, only as a means of deepening repentance, and as a test of its genuineness.

3. The Church of Rome permits at least, the addition of Direction to Confession, namely, the laying bare of heart and motives, that the Priest may guide the life.

Believing in the desirability of confession, accepting, too, the principle of such necessary guidance as scrupulous persons may require, or extraordinary contingencies demand ; I abhor the very notion of "*Direction.*"

4. The Church of Rome *enforces* confession ; the Church of England makes it *voluntary* ; and so do I.

5. And most important, the Church of Rome regards *confession as necessary to the forgiveness of sins* and *therefore* enforces it.

The Church of England, on the other hand, regards the voluntariness of confession as a necessary element in its usefulness, because, though often necessary to penitence and relief of the burdened soul, it *is not necessary to the forgiveness of sins* ; and as the Church teaches, so do I.

Do I need say more upon this subject ? Let me ask you to consider that the only proof which has been brought forward on this floor of these unfair statements, is an accusation that in 1870 or thereabouts, I heard certain confessions at Nashotah ; the object being to show that I intruded into the care of souls, and usurped a jurisdiction to which I had no right.

Mr. President, to accuse me of wrong towards Nashotah, is

like "seething a kid in its mother's milk." I came to this Diocese, from home and friends, a newly ordained Deacon, drawn hither by the saintly story of Nashotah House. For five years I was a tutor there, and reorganized the Preparatory Department, which was a very necessary part of the work of the Seminary. In 1859 I moved to Racine College, which for about ten years after continued to be the Preparatory Department of Nashotah.

I was bound to Nashotah by every tie. I had given it love, labour and self denial. The youths to whom I had been father, friend and pastor, and whom I loved as my own soul, and they me, were there as candidates. Was it surprising that now and then, one whom I had trained and guided should look to me for spiritual help. In the course of years there came one or two others, who were recommended to me by their own pastors, and at last two who perhaps could not be thus classified. The Rev. Dr. Cole, then and now President and Pastor of Nashotah, has informed you on this floor, that whatever I did, *I did with his knowledge, consent and approval*, and that I did no wrong. Do I need further justification? If so, I hold in my possession the whole correspondence which the unnecessary interference of Dr. Adams caused, and am prepared if need be to publish it.* It is somewhat difficult for one not versed in this sort of controversy to know what all this, even if true was intended to prove against me. The point of the whole accusation is to be found in the story told by Dr. Adams, that a student at Nashotah had refused to recite not to himself, but to some other professor, on the ground that his "*Director*" had told him not to do so. But, Mr. President, a classmate of the gentleman sits before us, and has just borne witness that the statement is incorrect, and the President of the institution has also informed us, that he too had examined the statement in question, and found the facts not to be as alleged. If *I* am meant by the Director in question, let me say that the story, so far as I am concerned, is a dream of my Brother's imagination, and that I have in my possession a letter of the young man himself, now an estimable clergyman of the Church, denying it in *toto*.

I have only one thing to add in conclusion that in the un-

*See Appendix v.

certain state of the practice of the church in regard to Confession, I long ago adopted certain principles for my guidance.

1. Not to hear the Confessions of minors without the consent of their parents, not even allowing a lad in my own College to make a Confession even if he desired to do so, if his parents forbade.

2. Not to hear the Confession of a wife, ordinarily, without the consent of her husband.

3. Not to hear Confessions in the Parishes of other clergymen, under ordinary circumstances, without their wish and consent.

I dare say that to the minds of many such a statement will only provoke censure. There is a large class to whom the mere word Confession is enough. It is easy to raise a hue and cry against it. But remember when you do so, that the loving care of our Mother the Church in this respect has trained many a noble soul to higher deeds of faith, and taught them to sorrow much, that they might have much forgiven, and having much forgiven to love the more.

PURGATORY.

There are two other charges in the Document. One of them has not even been mentioned on this floor, and not a solitary proof has been given for it. It sounded well, however to speak of " Prayers for the dead with a direct reference to PURGATORY, in the case of the most 'advanced men.' " Since my accusers do not defend it themselves, I only need to deny it. The second is

THE INVOCATION OF SAINTS AND ANGELS.

For proof of this a somewhat singular line of argument is adopted.

1. A certain young man joined the church of Rome.

2. This young man had a copy of the "Treasury of Devotion" given him by myself.

3. The " Treasury of Devotion" has certain prayers in it,* which by dexterious twisting, may be made to mean Invocation

*See Appendix vi.

of Saints and Angels, therefore the Rev. Dr. DeKoven believes in the Invocation of saints and angels. Q. E. D.

It seems absolutely pitiful that one should have to answer such arguments.

But in reply:

1. The gentleman in question is not a member of the Church of Rome, but is I am told a lay reader of the Episcopal Church in the Diocese of Illinois.

2. Being placed for a brief space of time, in the way of helping this person, and seeing him use a somewhat worn copy of the "Treasury of Devotion," I replaced it with a new one.

Permit me to ask, in this connection, whether a man necessarily pledges himself to every statement in a devotional book which he gives away. In my youth Baxter's "Saints Rest," Wilberforce's "Practical view," Doddridge's "Rise and Progress" and Hannah More's "Practical Piety" were favorite gifts. Did one become thereby an endorser of all in them. Have those persons, clerical and lay, who for many years have given away the Prayer Book with the old collection of Psalms and Hymns, become responsible for the doubtful doctrine some of the hymns contained. May one not present an unabridged edition of Thomas à Kempis, best and holiest of Books, and yet not quite endorse all his Eucharistic expressions. But,

3. The "Treasury of Devotion" is a slandered Book. It is edited by the Rev. T. T. Carter, one of the holiest Priests of the Church of England. The third edition has the following endorsement.

PALM SUNDAY, 1869.

"I have looked through your book and have begun to use it. In fact, I feel that I am now in a position to do more than acknowledge your gift: I thank you heartily for it, and assure you that it is to me a blessed thought that one, who was one of my own clergy, should now give me such effectual help to prepare for my account. May God bless you and keep you in your blessed work. This is the hearty prayer and wish of your affectionate brother in Christ,   W. K. SARUM."

This letter was written in the fourth month of his illness, rather more than four months before his death, by the saintly Bishop Hamilton, of Salisbury, now at rest with God.

The prayers alluded to are all of them prayers to Almighty

God that the intercessions of His Saints may help us. They are not prayers *to the Saints*, but simply *prayers to God.* Does any one doubt that these intercessions are offered. From this angry war of words, and bitter strife, I turn my thoughts away, to that land where the "wicked cease from troubling and the weary are at rest." I hear that ceaseless tide of prayer, that aweful swell of liturgic worship, that from the saints beneath the altar is upward borne, while the ministering angels pour the "vials full of odours which are the prayers of Saints." The weary earth is shaking to and fro. The divided Church is racked and torn by cruel dis-sension, but far "beyond these voices," in one united suppli-cation, checked by no discord, harmed by no schism, goes up the cry, "Lord, how long !" May I not ask of God to give me the benefit of this ceaseless intercession of the Church at rest, and yet be not charged with invoking the Saints? Does the Prayer Book invoke the angels when it prays, on St. Michael's day, "Grant that as Thy holy angels always do Thee service in Heaven, they may by Thy appointment, so succour and defend us on Earth." Is all this anything more than a belief in the grand old doctrine of the Communion of Saints? And this is all that the Treasury of Devotion can be accused of.

But in conclusion, let me ask, Mr. President, are these things after all the dangers of the Church of Wisconsin? Do we need to warn our people against Confession, Eucharistical Adora-tion, and too much reverence? Is Milwaukee full of penitents? Are the rural districts of Wisconsin inclined to superstition? Must I say, that even I, who am supposed to embody all this idea of over much religion; outside of my own College, and some few directly or indirectly connected with it, as before mentioned; have never heard the confession of a lay man or a lay woman in the whole Diocese of Wisconsin. Nay, under whatever circum-stances I have been thrown in a ministry of nearly 20 years, out-side of the same limits, I have not heard the Confessions of more than twenty persons, clerical and lay, in this whole land. The average of one a year may be surely sufficiently exceptional.

My Brethren, I see before me the mighty work the Church of God might do. I hear the cries of pain and anguish that go up to Heaven. This terrible record of crime and misery, this story of lost and ruined souls, we do not save, rends my heart. I know that the chief dangers of the day do not lie in too many confessions, or over wrought devotion, or too high an appreciation of the Sacraments of the Church. They are rather to be found in unbelief and sin, in corruption and dishonour, in covetousness, lust and irreverence, in inaction, and stagnation, and quaking timidity, and ye all know it !

But from such thoughts as these, from all that has passed in these sad days, from a bitterness I have not deserved, nay, even from these warm hearts whose human sympathy has sustained me in this, my time of trial, I turn myself away. I lift my heart to Him on Whose Almighty Arm I lean, and in Whose mighty power even my weakness is strong, and louder than the din of angry words, nay, because of the prayers that so many have lovingly prayed, I hear the gracious promise :

"Commit thy way unto the Lord, and He will bring it to pass."

" He will make thy righteousness as clear as the light, and thy just dealing as the noon day."

APPENDIX.

———o———

I.

Rev. James DeKoven, D. D.,
>*Rev. and Dear Brother:*

Will you permit the undersigned your brothers in the Holy Ministry; who have known you intimately for many years and regard you with unfeigned love and admiration; and who are persuaded that some of your opinions and practices as a priest in this church are much misunderstood, and in some cases we fear uncharitably misrepresented, to ask you respectfully and in the interests of truth and peace the following questions?

1. Are you, or have you ever been a member of the Society called the "Confraternity of the Blessed Sacrament?"

2. Do you believe in any other than a Spiritual Presence of the Body and Blood of our Lord in the Holy Eucharist; or that worship can be lawfully paid to the material elements in that Sacrament?" .

3. Do you regard high ritual in public worship as generally desirable or necessary?

4. Do you believe confession to a priest to be necessary to the forgiveness of sins; or necessary as a preliminary to the due reception of the Holy Communion?

We do not ask these questions for the sake of being ourselves convinced that you hold no views which the wise liberality of our church does not tolerate; or that you encourage no usages either in your public or private ministrations which she does not allow. For of this we are already convinced. While we do not, as you are well aware, adopt the form of words in which you have publicly expressed an honest and allowed opinion, we would not, if we could, deny to you that liberty in this or in any other respect, which every portion of the Catholic and Apostolic Church has ever granted, and (with the exception of the Church of Rome since the Vatican Council) still grants to her children; a liberty which, as it seems to us, some of our Brethren who demand and enjoy it without suspicion or censure themselves, are unwilling to accord to all to whom the Church accords it.

Our purpose in asking these questions is, that we may, with your consent give such publicity to your answers as truth and justice, and the welfare of the Church of which you are an honoured and influential Presbyter may seem to require.

Having often conversed with you on the points they cover, we are assured that your answers will disabuse many of the suspicions which we believe to be unfounded, and put an end to imputations, which we are persuaded neither your opinions nor your practices justify.

With sentiments of great respect and warm affection we remain your brothers in Christ and the Church,

WM. BLISS ASHLEY,	WILLIAM DAFTER,
W. ALEXADER FALK,	FAYETTE ROYCE,

———

The Rev. Dr. Ashley, The Rev. Mr. Dafter. The Rev. Dr. Falk, The Rev. Mr. Royce.

My Dear Brethren .

I thank you very much for your kind letter, and am glad to say anything I can, which may serve to lessen the misconstruction of which you write.

1. I am not, and never have been, a member of the Society called the "Confraternity of the Blessed Sacrament," nor in any way connected therewith.

I ought not therefore to be held responsible by any reasonable person for the acts or words of this Society, be they good or bad.

2. With regard to the Holy Eucharist, I hold the views of many of the older Divines of the Church of England—and especially of Bishop Andrewes—surely one of the greatest of them; and in our own day of such men as Bishop Forbes of the Scotch Church, the late Bishop Hamilton of Salisbury, of Dr. Liddon, the learned theologian and eloquent preacher, of Dr. Pusey, and of John Keble, the saintly author of the "Christian Year."

Believing in the presence of the Body and Blood of the Lord in the Consecrated Elements I believe that Presence to be in no sense *material* or *corporeal*, but *spiritual*: though none the less real and true, because spiritual.

I think it would be idolatry to be abhorred of any christian man, to worship the material Elements; nor would I worship the Body and Blood of Christ in the Elements, as subsisting (were this possible) apart from his Divine Person. In the words of Bishop Andrewes, however,

"Assuredly Christ Himself the substance of the Sacrament (Res Sacramenti) *in* and *with* the Sacrament (Sacramentum) out of and without the Sacrament, wheresoever He is, is to be adored."

In thus worshipping Christ in the Eucharist, inasmuch as this worship is addressed to His Divine Person, it would not be addressed as though he were, or could be, confined to the Holy Elements.

Nor do I hold this view as though I had the right to condemn those who might not be able to receive it; as I am well aware that on this sacred and mysterious subject, the Church has seen fit to tolerate a certain latitude of view, forbidddidg only Transubstantiation on the one side, and Zwinglianism on the other.

3. With regard to ritual, I believe that every national Church has the right to regulate the outward worship of her children. Whensoever she commands, it is the duty of her children to obey. Any ritual moreover which expresses a doctrine the Church condemns is wrong. Within these limits I think there should be for those who need it a lofty ceremonial, and for others the simplest services. The Church should be elastic enough to admit of both· Place, circumstances, and needs will cause the amount of ceremonial to vary, for beyond all ritual is charity to souls, and that ritual is the best which brings most sinners to Christ.

4. With respect to the Confession of Sins to God in the presence of a Priest, I hold that the Prayer Book in certain specified cases provides for and encourages it. Nor am I able to accept what seems to me to be an illogical deduction, that because the church advises it in certain cases she therefore necessarily forbids it in all others.

At the same time I firmly hold that private confession is neither necessary to the forgiveness of sins, nor a necessary preliminary to the Holy Communion, nor to be enforced upon any one. Indeed I regard the voluntariness of Confession as an absolute necessity to its ever being of any use to a sin-laden soul.

Your questions so far as they are doctrinal do not cover of course the whole range of these important subjects, and my answers are necessarily limited to the range they involve.

I have abstained from answering newspaper attacks upon me, partly because I had the hope, that one born and brought up in the Church, and whose whole life, with a ministry of now nearly twenty years, has been honestly devoted to its service, might need no defence from charges of disloyalty and dishonour; and partly because in all such controversies, one is quite at the mercy of either the paper or its anonymous correspondents.

It seems right, however, when my Brethren ask it of me, that I should speak, lest by my silence the cause of the truth should suffer.

Thanking you for your kindness to me

I am most truly your friend and servant,

JAMES DE KOVEN.

II.

The following is the Document entitled "Principles, not Men," as sent out before the Council, to the Diocese of Wisconsin. The correspondence contained in Appendix I. was not printed as a reply to it, nor was this document a reply to that correspondence. They appeared at the same time. I beg to call the reader's especial attention to the portion of the document printed in italics. For the following reason. In the *Church Journal* of March 5th, the editor professed to publish this document, "as a very clear and able setting out of the differences between "High" Churchmen and self-styled "Catholics" . . . . . . "for preservation and for a land-mark " But he does not state that he published an expurgated edition. The words in italics are the parts omitted. It is no slight testimony to their character that even the *Church Journal* is ashamed of them. *But what shall be said of the fact that the Document is published without the slightest hint being given that it is not the original paper, and that the editor has appended the names of the gentlemen who signed it, (though one had publicly withdrawn his name,) as though it were the paper they had originally signed :*

" PRINCIPLES—NOT MEN."

The Chicago Times of Saturday last, gives large space to an account of the interview held by its reporter, with certain of the clergy and laity of the Diocese of Wisconsin, relative to the approaching election of a Bishop. Presuming that the report is accurate, I desire to make some remarks upon it.

The Rev. Dr. De Koven evidently had the skill to put his case in the best light. Had the reporter been previously instructed to avoid all embarrassing questions, and to give him the fullest oppptunity to extricate himself from an untenable position, he could not have put his interrogaries in a more favorable manner. The one point brought up was the Eucharistic speech of Dr. De Koven in the last General Convention, and he immediately explained that it had been misunderstood and misrepresented, &c. But questions concerning the confessional, prayers for the dead, purgatory, the invocation of saints, the propitiatory sacrifice of the Eucharist, and other well known tenets of the Ritualistic party were carefully avoided.

There was also throughout the whole report, the assumption that there are but two parties in the Episcopal Church, the High Church and Low Church. Dr. De Koven claimed to be a high churchman of the "advanced" type; and the contest was represented as one only of men, and not of principles.

But with all due respect to Dr. De Koven, this classification cannot be permitted to pass. If the question about the succession to the Episcopate of Wisconsin were only between two high churchmen, it would not create a tithe of the interest that is felt in it all over the Church. The non-existence of a low church party in Wisconsin makes the election of a high churcnman—if there be no other party—a foregone conclusion, and Dr. De Koven is not so remarkable a man, personally, that his candidacy, apart from other considerations, would attract the attention that is being given to one of the poorest dioceses in the Church.

The classification used to be high church and low church ; but within a few years a third party has sprung up, distinct from either, which arrogates to itself the name of the Catholic party; but which is known by others as the Ritualistic party. Now the great interest felt in the Wisconsin election, is due entirely to the fact, that it is known to be a question between the high church and ritualistic parties. We cannot therefore permit the differences between these parties to be ignored. They are fundamental, and make, as we say, two distinct parties, and not two wings of the same party.

Outside of the Apostles' and Nicene creeds which are common to all parties, the distinctive principles of the high church party are the following :

1. That the Church is a divine organization.

2. That the ministry is traced back in the line of Apostolic succession, in a threefold order of bishops, priests and deacons.

3. Baptismal regeneration and sacramental grace.

The distinctive principles of the Ritualistic party are :

1. The presence of Christ "in the elements, on the altar," after the consecration of the bread and wine.

2. The use of vestments, lights, incense, &c., as accessories of Eucharistic adoration.

3. Auricular confession as having a sacramental character ; and therefore useful for all Christians as an ordinary means of the forgiveness of sins.

4. Prayers for the dead, with a direct reference to purgatory, in the case of the most "advanced" men.

5. The invocation of saints and angels.

The high churchman charges the ritualists with "Romanizing," because of the above tenets. The ritualist, on the contrary, sneers at the high churchmen as "high-and-dry," because he will not "advance" with him in the direction of Rome. The parties are distinct in their principles and their aims.

The text books of the high churchmen are the divines of the 16th and 17th centuries : Pearson, Bull, Hooker, Andrewes, &c., and the Fathers of the Primitive Church.

The text books of the ritualist are the writings of Pusey, Newman, Keble, R. I. Wilberforce, the volume of Gerard Cobb, entitled the "Kiss of Peace, or England and Rome at One," &c. Mohler's "Symbolik," and the scholastic divines and ritualists of the Middle Ages, translations and synopses of which, issue every now and then from the press of this party.

As the two parties are distinct in principle, so are they in practice.

The practical results of high church teaching are :

1. That baptised persons, being members of the church, are led to realize their calling and responsibilities as "a royal priesthood, a holy nation, a peculiar people."

2. That the threefold ministry of apostolic succession is exclusive of Popes on the one side, and of unauthorized teachers on the other.

3. That the sacramental union of the faithful with their risen Lord is at once the means and the call to holiness of heart and life.

The practical results of ritualistic teachings are :

1. That the eucharistic service is to be assimilated in its outward semblance, as much as possible, to the mass celebrated in Roman Catholic churches, by means of the accessories of lights, music, vestments, incense, postures, genuflexions and adorations.

2. That non-recipients are to be present at the eucharistic service, for the purpose of being benefited by the sacrifice, and of directing acts of adoration to the presence in the elements on the altar.

3. That members of the church are to be persuaded, as an ordinary and frequent thing, to come to auricular confession and to put their consciences in "holy obedience," under the priest's "direction."

4. That the eucharist is to be offered, as a propitiatory sacrifice for the living and the dead.

5. That prayers for the dead, and the invocation of saints and angels are to be practised.

These being the differences between the high church and ritualistic parties, it is evident what must be the interest felt in the Wisconsin election, when the candidate, who was claimed by the ritualistic party in the Massachusetts election, the Rev. Dr. De Koven, is put forward in the diocese in which he resides The Wisconsin election is a test of the relative strength of the high church and ritualistic parties, in a diocese in which there is no low church party to help it against the ritualists.

Now accepting the Rev. Dr. De Koven's explanation of his position, as given in the
Times report, it still remains true that Dr. De Koven is identified with the ritualistic party,
by his adoption of the words of Mr. Bennett, in the celebrated English trial, and his en-
trenchment of himself behind them in "adjudicated words."

Dr. De Koven avows a presence to be adored in the elements on the altar. He claims
that this is within the limits of opinion allowed by the church. But Dr. De Koven knows as
well as anyone that no article, rubric, line or word, authorizes him to set forth that opinion
as a doctrine of the church. All that the adjudication amounts to, is that a man who holds
this as his private opinion, is not therefore suspended or excommunicated, but for the present
tolerated.

Dr. De Koven holds his right to enter any pulpit of the Episcopal Church, only by the
commission given him to teach "as our Lord hath commanded, and as this church hath received the same." But this church has given no sign in any of her authorized formularies,
that she has "received" a revelation of a presence to be adored in the elements on the altar.

Still it may be argued on behalf of Dr. De Koven and the ritualists, that this is a merely
speculative opinion, especially as the Doctor explicitly disavows a belief in transubstatiation.
But unfortunately the practical results of this belief, are identical with the practical results of
transubstantiation, and the difference is merely speculative and nugatory as between his belief and that of the Church of Rome. For the acts of adoration addressed to the presence in
the elements on the altar, are precisely those addressed by the members of the Church of
Rome to the host, and none other. This localization of the presence implies an arrangement
of the service, with lights, vestments, prostrations, non-communicant adorations, a reserved
sacrament, processions of Corpus Christi, and all other incidents with which the attendants
upon Roman Catholic worship are familiar, and which are foreign to our own "use." It implies an offering of Christ by the priest for the living and the dead—it implies in every respect,
what the ritualists call it, the mass, and not the Holy Communion.

Dr. De Koven, again, is known to recommend and practice auricular confession. In
this also, he and his party make a distinction to ward off the charge of Romanizing, which
is void of any practical result in distinguishing his theology from that of Rome. The distinction he makes is, that confession with him is voluntary, while with the Romanist it is enforced. But if confession be of that advantage which Dr. De Koven and the ritualistic party,
with the church of Rome, believe, they cannot consistently and conscientiously rest until they
have made it enforced and not voluntary. For to leave their flocks without so great a benefit, for the want of its enforcement, must be, according to their view, a dereliction of duty.
Their position with respect to the confessional is only provisional, and not final, and the "advanced" man in this direction, must necessarily be an "advancing" man, until he stands
fairly and squarely with the Church of Rome.

With respect to the invocation of saints, and prayers for the dead, the position of the
party *and of Dr. De Koven*, is not uncertain, though less is said about these things, until
they have made sure of their position upon the mass and the confessional.

*If Dr. De Koven is made Bishop of Wisconsin, the necessary tendency of his princi-
ples and associations will be to require an arrangement of the Episcopal Cathedral, identical with that of Bishop Henni's Cathedral; the altar must be decorated with lights;
the priest must be dressed in vestments, the people must prostrate themselves at the elevation of the host, the confessional boxes must line the walls, the people will not know
whether they are in the one or the other. And if Dr De Koven be held back from this,
by the necessity of conceding to the public opinion of his clergy and laity, he must feel
trammelled and uncomfortable in the position he will hold, and the restraint will be the
more irksome, the more honest and earnest he is.*

I have written this, Mr. Editor, not out of any unfriendly feeling for Dr. De Koven, of
whose honesty and sincerity I have the highest appreciation; but because I believe Dr. De
Koven to be advancing in a wrong direction, and being so, to be in greater danger, the more
honest and sincere he is. A dishonest man can be inconsistent, an honest man cannot. And
I want the High Churchmen of this Diocese, if they are led by Dr. De Koven's great person-
popularity to give him their vote, to see just what they are doing. The High Church

party and the Ritualistic party are *toto cælo* apart, and if Dr. De Koven permits himself to be identified with the latter, we, who are of the former, must let no personal affection or admiration for him blind us to the possible consequences.

.

A systematic attempt has been made to give the impression that in the approaching election of a Bishop for this Diocese, the question to be settled is simply one of men, not of doctrines and principles. The undersigned do not so regard it. They have seen an article in the Milwaukee papers of January 31st, which they think sets forth correctly the points to be decided in the coming election. They have reprinted it in its present form for general circulation in the Diocese, as a document well calculated to give a right view of the issues involved in the present contest.

February 2d, 1874.

Signed,

LEWIS A. KEMPER D. D., *Professor of Hebrew and Biblical Literature at Nashotah, and Rector of St. Paul's Church, Ashippun.*

WILLIAM ADAMS, D. D., *Professor of Systematic Divinity at Nashotah.*

JOHN H. EGAR, D. D., *Professor of Ecclesiastical History, Nashotah.*

ROBERT N. PARKE, *Rector of Trinity Church, Oshkosh.*

JOHN WILKINSON, *Rector of Grace Church, Madison.*

MARISON BYLLESBY, *Rector of St. James Church, Milwaukee.*

———o———

III.

An attempt has been made in the *Churchman* of Feb. 7, 1874, to prove that Bishop Andrewes did not believe in the presence of the *Person of our Lord Jesus Christ*, in Sacramental Union with the Elements after Consecration. The article as a whole is directed against a circular of the "Confraternity of the Blessed Sacrament," and I only propose to treat of this point and of the phrase "under the form of bread and wine," leaving the rest untouched. The paragraph is as follows—I quote from the *Churchman:*

" What does Bishop Andrewes teach on this subject? In his sermon VII, on the Resurrection, he is speaking of what we receive in receiving the Consecrated Elements, and he expresses the act of receiving by the word *Epulemur.* He then says, "Will ye mark one thing more, that *epulemur* doth here refer to *immolatus?* To Christ not every way considered, but as when he was offered. *Christ's Body that now is.* True, but not Christ's *as now it is*, but as then it was,when it was offered, rent and slain, and sacrificed for us. *Not as now He is glorified;* for *so* He is not, cannot be *immolatus,* for he is immortal and impassible. But as then He was when he suffered death; that is passible and mortal. Then in His passible estate, did He institute this of ours to be a memorial of his Passible and Passio both. And we are in this action *not only carried up to Christ* (sursum corda) but we are also carried back to Christ, as He was at the very instant and in the very act of His offering. So and no otherwise doth this text teach. So and no otherwise do we represent Him. By the incomprehensible power of the Holy Spirit, *not He alone,* but He, as at the very act of His offering, is made present to us, and we incorporate into His death, and invested in the benefits of it. If an host could be turned into Him, now glorified as he is, it would not serve : Christ offered is it—thither we must look. To the serpent lift up, thither we must repair, even *ad cadavera;* we must, *hoc facere,* do that is then done. So, and no otherwise, is this *epulare* to be conceived: And so, I think *none will say* they do or can turn Him." [Sermons, Vol. ii, page 306.]

Leaving the Latin words in italics of course, I have ventured to alter the italics of the *Churchman* and to put some of my own. I do this to show that whatever views Bishop Andrewes held about the Sacrifice, they did not *exclude the idea of the Presence of Christ's Glorified Body* in Sacramental Union with the Consecrated Elements. This fact is evident from this very quotation. I purpose to show from other quotations that it does not admit of a doubt. The writer in the *Churchman* goes on:

" Now this teaching is distinct. It shows that Andrewes held that the body and blood in the Eucharist were "*the Crucified Flesh of Christ,* and not *His Glorified Person;*" and since this flesh, *qua,* crucified is not in actual being, it is present, not in substance, but in a mystery and representatively: *i.e.* "in *spiritual power* not by *material contact.*"

In the passage the quotation marks and the italics are those of the writer in the *Churchman*.

Of course the ordinary reader would suppose that the quotation marks showed that the *passages quoted were from Bishop Andrewes*. This however is not the case   They are to be found in a little book styled " Sacrifice and Participation of the Holy Eucharist" by Canon Trevor, published in 1869 (see p. 90, also pp. 72 and 73), and are in part as foreign to the teaching of Bishop Andrewes, as they are to the teaching of antiquity.

I purpose now to show what Bishop Andrewes really taught. To this end I will venture myself to quote the book of Canon Trevor, p. 15.

" To the first article of this Decree (Decree of the Council of Trent concerning the Sacrifice of the Mass) the objections may be reduced to a question of words rather than things. The ' Body and Blood' of Christ, mean in Scripture and in all Catholic Antiquity, the crucified Body, and outshed Blood of the Sacrifice of the Cross; and it is admitted by Roman Catholic Divines that in this condition they are not really contained in the Sacrament but are repre sented by it.   Consequently notwithstanding the expressions ' under the forms of bread and wine,' the Sacrifice according to the ar.icle is only ' *representative* of the Sacrifice of the Cross, and applicatory of its virtue ;' an application undoubtedly made to the faithful in partaking of the Communion."

Canon Trevor proves this assertion in regard to Roman Catholic Divines, by two quotations, one from Cardinal Cajetan, and the other from Cardinal Perron, as follows:

"The Sacrament is not really the Body of Christ constituted in the actual state of one slain, dead and inanimate ; neither in that respect does it contain it, but so far represents it only." [Cardinal Perron, de loc. Aug. iii.] [Patrick's Full View, 213.]

I quote the passage from Canon Trevor not as endorsing the words "The Body and Blood of Christ mean in Scripture and in all Catholic Antiquity, the crucified Body and outshed Blood of the Sacrifice of the Cross," and that alone; but simply to show what the view of Roman Catholic Divines and of Cardinal Perron in particular was upon the subject of the Sacrifice.

In the same way Bishop Buckeridge in the funeral sermon he preached for Bishop Andrewes, quotes Thomas Aquinas to the same effect, as saying:

" That this Sacrament is called a Sacrifice inasmuch as it doth *represent* the Passion of Christ; it is likewise called *Hostia*, an ' host ' inasmuch as it containeth Christ Himself, who is *Hostia Salutaris*."

No one will suppose for a moment that these Roman Catholic Divines did not hold "that the Body and Blood of Christ together with the Soul and Divinity of our Lord Jesus Christ, and consequently the whole Christ," are present after consecration.

My argument thus far is simply to show, not that Bishop Andrewes agreed in all respects with these Roman Divines on the Eucharist; no one could have more earnestly denied Transubstantiation than he; but that it is not *incompatible* to hold the two things as present, Christ's Body as slain *representatively*, and Christ's *Glorified Person*.

I will now advance one step further and assert that in the matter of the Sacrifice, Bishop Andrewes did not disagree with this very Cardinal Perron whom Canon Trevor quotes.   In his answer to Cardinal Perron the bishop says in remarkable language:

"V. THE EUCHARIST A SACRIFICE. 6.

" 1. The Eucharist ever was and by us is considered both as a *Sacrament*, and as a *Sacrifice*.

" 2. A *Sacrifice* is proper and appliable only *to divine worship*.

" 3. The *Sacrifice of Christ's death did succeed to the Sacrifices of the Old Testament*.

" 4. The Sacrifice of Christ's death is available for present, absent, living, dead, (yea, for them that are yet *unborn*'.

" 5. When we say the *dead*, we mean it is available for the *Apostles*, *Martyrs*, and Confessors, and all (because we are all members of one Body ;) THESE NO MAN WILL DENY.

" 6. In a word we hold with St. Augustine in the same chapter which the Cardinal citeth, '*quod hujus sacrificii Caro et Sanguis, ante Adventum Christi, per victimas similitudinum promittebatur ; in passione Christi, per ipsam veritatem reddabatur ; post adventum* (leg. *ascensum*,) *Christi, per Sacramentum memoria celebratur*." (pp. 19 and 20 of Bishop Andrewes' Minor Works, Anglo Cath. Lib.]

The small capitals are my own, the italics are Bishop Andrewes and are intended to show, I suppose, the points of agreement between himself and the Cardinal.

In the summary at the end of the answer to the 18th chapter of Cardinal Perron's reply (p. 35 of the same) in summing up the points of agreement and difference between himself and the Church of England on the one hand, and Cardinal Perron on the other, he mentions the Eucharistic sacrifice *as a point on which they agree.*

In his reply to Cardinal Bellarmine also he says (p. 251 of the Responsio. Angl. Cath. Lib):

"Take you away from the Mass your Transubstantiation and we shall not long quarrel about the *Sacrifice.*"

Agreeing therefore with Cardinal Perron and Cardinal Bellarmine as to the Sacrifice, though he denied Transubstantiation, it is evident that no remark of Bishop Andrewes, in regard to the Sacrifice, can be used to show that he *necessarily* therefore disbelieved in our Lord's Personal Presence in Sacramental Union with the Holy Elements.

Bishop Andrewes was too great a theologian to be content with the one sided view of the presence of Christ, merely as slain. He knew that if "Christ died for our sins " " He rose again also for our justification." According to his view Christ himself the inward part of the Sacrament was present in Sacramental union with the Holy Elements, in two aspects, as risen and glorified, as well as the "Lamb as it had been slain."

On this subject there is positive proof.

1. In the xvi Sermon on the Nativity (vol. i, of the Angl. Cath. Lib. pp. 282 and 283,) already quoted in this defence, p. 14, Bishop Andrewes compares, as he does also again in other places, the union of the sign with the thing signified in the Holy Eucharist, to the union of the Divine and Human Natures in the one Person of our Lord Jesus Christ. He uses the argument negatively against Transubstantiation, and positively for the Sacramental union of the sign and the thing signified, by means of consecration and before reception.

2. The thing signified, *signatum, res Sacramenti,* is with Bishop Andrewes. not merely the Body and Blood of Christ, but *"Christ Himself."*

In the famous passage on Eucharistic adoration, already given in full. (p. 22–24,) which the *Churchman* did not allude to, he says:

"*Christ Himself the inward part of the Sacrament,* in and with the Sacrament, out of and without the Sacrament, wheresoever he is, is to be adored."

Let it be noted also that this statement is from a controversial Treatise, and not merely from a Sermon.

So too in the xvi Sermon on the Nativity, from which we have just quoted, he says:

"For there (in the Holy Mysteries) we do not gather to Christ, nor of Christ, but we gather *Christ Himself,* and *gathering Him,* we shall gather the tree and fruit and all upon it."

So too in the xii Sermon of the Nativity (pp 213 and 214, vol. i, Angl. Cath. Lib.):

"The Sacrament we shall have besides, and if the Sacrament we may well say, *Hoc erit signum.* For a sign it is, and by it, *invenietis Puerum,* 'ye shall find this child.' For finding His flesh and blood ye cannot miss but *find Him too.* And a sign not much from this here. For Christ in the Sacrament is not altogether unlike Christ in the cratch. To the cratch we may well liken the husk or outward symbols of it. Outwardly it seems of little worth, but it is rich of contents, as was the crib this day with Christ in it. For what are they but *infirma et egena elementa* 'weak and poor elements of themselves ?' Yet in THEM FIND WE CHRIST. Even as they did this day *in præsepi jumentorum panem angelorum,* "in the beasts crib the food of angels," which very food our signs both *represent and present.*"

And lastly and conclusively in the 9th Sermon of the Resurrection (vol.ii, Angl. Cath. Lib., p. 340,):

" Not to do it (bow) at His name ? Not at the Holy Mysteries themselves, not to do it. Where His name is, I am sure and more than His name, even the Body and Blood of our Lord Jesus Christ ; and these NOT WITHOUT HIS SOUL ; NOR THAT WITHOUT HIS DEITY ; nor all these without inestimable high benefits of grace attending on them."

Therefore with Bishop Andrewes in His thanksgiving after the communion (see devotions) we will pray.

" It is finished and done, so far as in our power, Christ our God, the mystery of Thy dispensation. For we have held remembrance of Thy death, we have seen the figure of thy Resurrection, we have been filled with Thy endless life."

In the article in question there is also a criticism upon the phrase "under the form of bread and wine."

Bishop Andrewes says:

" The terms *sous les especes* or *dans les especes sacramentales* (under the forms) it would pose the Cardinal (Perron) and all the whole college to find they were ever heard or dreamt of in St. Augustine's time or many hundred years afterwards." [Minor Works, p. 14, Lib. Angl. Cath. Theo.]

The quotation is a correct one. But it must be noticed that it is no argument against the use of the words in a proper way Cardinal Perron uses them in proof of Transubstantiation. Bishop Andrewes replies they do not prove it because they are not ancient words. He took the Cardinal's terms in the sense in which the Cardinal used them, of accidents of which the substance was gone. In this sense the phrase " under the form of bread and wine " is equivalent to Transubstantiation; and in this sense I have not used it. There is authority for it however in the Church of England in the true sense, as denoting a spiritual Presence in Sacramental Union with the Holy Elements.

Down to the beginning of the fifteenth century while it was held that the " Body of Christ is truly and principally in the Sacrament under the form of bread and wine," it was still an open question whether the substance of bread remained or no. Cranmer and Ridley were familiar with the expression in the writings of Bertram as denoting a Presence, the substance of bread and wine still remaining. Used and disused in the reign of Henry VIII, Cranmer and the other Bishops brought back the language at the end of the first Book of Homilies. "Hereafter shall follow sermons of the Nativity, Passion, Resurrection, and Ascension of our Saviour Christ; of the due receiving of His *Blessed Body and Blood under the form of bread and wine* " And after the interval of the reign of Queen Mary, the Bishops in the beginning of the reign of Elizabeth, refer to that notice in the title to the second Book of Homilies, "of such matters as were promised and *entituled* in the former Book of Homilies." Nor will it do to dispose of this matter in the cavalier way in which Canon Trevor gets rid of it, by saying that it has only the authority of the King's Printer; and that the Homily when it appeared did not bear this title, (note p. 90,) for though the latter fact is true, the first Book of Homilies has since its publication been twice revised, but this *theological statement has not been interfered with.* The same form moreover appears in Queen Elizabeth's Primer, which was a revision of that of Henry VIII, and while one word was altered in the sentence in which the phrase " under the form of bread and wine " occurs, that phrase itself was not altered. The words are:

" Our Saviour and Redeemer, Jesu Christ, which in Thy Last Supper with thine Apostles didst deliver Thy *Blessed Body and Blood under the form of bread and wine.*" [Private Prayers set forth by authority during the reign of Queen Elizabeth, p. 87, Parker Society.]

It is true that the same Primer when printed again in 1566 dropped the phrase, but it occurs in varying senses in Bishop Nicholson's Treatise on the Catichism (p. 178, Angl. Cath. Lib.) in Sherlock's Practical Christian (p. 252, Oxford 1844,) and in Sutton's Godly Meditations on the Most Holy Sacrament of the Lord's Supper (p. 28, edition of 1844.)

Indeed Mr. Stephens, the counsel against Mr. Bennett, while arguing that the phrase as used in the English Church does not bear out Mr. Bennett's view, is constrained to acknowledge:

" It has not been contended by the Counsel in this case that the phrase ' under the form of bread and wine,' does *per se* express the doctrine of Transubstantiation ; but that the phrase has always expressed the doctrine of the real Presence of the Body and Blood of Christ in the Elements, which is a different doctrine from Transubstantiation." [Argument of A J. Stephens, Q. C. etc., in Shepard *vs.* Bennett, pp. 36 and 37.]

It must also be noted that both the Court of Arches and the Judicial Com mittee of the Privy Council decided that these words did not contravene the articles of the faith. As expressing the doctrine of the Real Presence and only so, have I used them.

Since writing the above I have read the editorial in the *Churchman* of March 14th upon Bishop Andrewes. The writer shows conclusively enough what Bishop Andrewes' views as to the Sacrifice were, and gives full quotations in proof.

To prove his second point, that Bishop Andrewes did not believe in the Presence of Christ's glorified Humanity, in Sacramental Union with the Holy Elements, the writer makes no allusion to any one of the quotations we have given; but simply repeats the solitary passage from Sermon vii on the Resurrection, quoted in the previous article, and which we have already answered. *Christ Himself* according to Bishop Andrewes is *the inward part of the Sacrament*, present as a Sacrifice representatively, present in His glorified Humanity, to feed us with Himself.

In Note C the Editor repeats the story, that the quotation made by myself in the General Convention was an incorrect quotation. The writer states this on the authority of the judgment in the case of Shepard *vs.* Bennett found in the work entitled *"Six Judgments, etc,"* and *"reprinted from an official copy."* The writer does not state, however, that Mr. Brooke's "Six Privy Council Judgments," nowhere gives the " Phillimore Judgment," for the simple reason that it was not a *judgment of the Privy Council at all,* but of the *Court of Arches.*

I could not, I must repeat, have quoted from the " Privy Council Judgement" in October, 1871, because it was *not delivered till June,* 1872. My quotation is taken from the "Judgement delivered by the Rt. Hon. Sir Robert Phillimore, D. C. L. Official Principal of the Arches Court of Canterbury, in the case of the office of the Judge promoted by Shepard *vs.* Bennett," edited by Walter G. F. Phillimore, B. C. L., the son of Sir Robert, and published by the Rivington's in 1870. The preface states that it is "published with the permission of the Judge." The second Edition of the Phillimore Judgement, published in 1871, when a year's time had been given to correct the mistake, if it were one, has the same words, and there is not the slightest reason to doubt their accuracy.

———o———

IV.
PRIVATE ABSOLUTION.

In the Document, "Principles, not Men," nothing is said about Absolution. Nothing, too, was said upon the floor of the House, except what I may nave said myself upon the subject. I might, therefore, pass it over, and yet it seems as if the subject were incompletely stated, without mentioning it.

It ought to be said, that it is generally believed, that the views of the three Professors are the same as my own on this subject, and it was a fact which was evident to all, that in attacking me on the subject of Confession, they did not object either to Confession or Absolution, but to their own travesty of what I hold, or to some supposed irregular exercise on my part of an undoubted function of the priestly office.

1. Let me say, that while I cannot but blush that the ignorance of people, and the want of fairness of much modern controversy should compel one to say it; I firmly believe that no one can forgive sins save Almighty God. To Him only doth it appertain. Nor in anything that I say about Absolution do I mean to limit the privilege of the sinner, to go with the burden of his sins directly to God, and in proportion to his penitence, receive forgiveness from his Father in Heaven.

2. I also believe that the *"Son of man* hath power *on earth* to forgive sins," and ordinarily exercises that power by His Priests and in His Sacra-

—56—

ments. I believe in "one baptism for the remission of sins." I believe that in the Holy Eucharist "we and all Thy whole Church obtain remission of our sins and all other benefits of His Passion." I hold too, in the words of the Homily of "Common Prayer and Sacraments," that absolution, "although no such Sacrament as Baptism and the Communion," still has *"the promise of the forgiveness of sin."*

I firmly believe also what our Lord said to His apostles and what the Church has said to her priests ever since, whatever form of words may be used in ordination, '·Whosoever sins ye remit they are remitted unto them, and whosoever sins ye retain they are retained." In other words, whenever God's ministers, in public or in private, in the two Sacraments or in Absolution, according to God's word, and on the conditions which He has prescribed, namely repentance and faith, tell a penitent that God forgives him, God confirms the word of His ambassadors and does forgive. In short, I do not believe all the solemn things the Bible and Prayer Book say about absolution, to be *a mere sham.* The form of words by which Absolution is pronounced is immaterial. It may be precatory, or indicative, or declaratory; the only point is that if it prays, God answers; if it indicates, it is God, not man who indicates; if it declares, the declaration carries with it, what the declaration implies. An individual Christian, a father, a mother, a friend, a teacher, does not hesitate under certain circumstances to assure a broken and contrite heart, that the merciful Father pardons him for Jesus' sake; and if one of the royal Priesthood can do so, much more, and with another and higher authority, the Priest who is set apart to do this very work.

I dare say that most Churchmen will agree with me thus far, I come now to the point of difficulty. Can a Priest in the American Church pronounce a private Absolution? I answer yes; and while I grant that the subject is a difficult one, I believe my reasons must satisfy any thoughtful Churchman.

The English Prayer Book says, as quoted in the Defence p. 35, that if a man's conscience is troubled he can go to his Minister, not only for counsel and advice, but also for the "benefit of Absolution." In the "Visitation of the sick," in the same Prayer Book, it is said, "Here shall the sick person be moved to make a special confession of his sins, if he feel his conscience troubled with any weighty matter, after which confession the priest shall absolve him (if he humbly and heartily desire it), after this sort :

"Our Lord Jesus Christ, who hath left power to His Church to absolve all sinners who truly repent and believe in Him, of His great mercy forgive thee thine offences : And by His authority committed to me, I absolve thee from all thy sins. In the name of the Father, and of the Son, and of the Holy Ghost—Amen.

But in the exhortation to the Communion in the American Prayer Book, the words "benefit of absolution" are omitted, and the rubric in the Visitation of the Sick is also left out, and the following rubric retained :

" Then shall the minister examine whether he repent him truly of his former sins, and be in charity with all the world, exhorting him to forgive from the bottom of his heart all persons that have offended him, and if he hath offended any other, to ask them forgiveness ; and where he hath done injury or wrong to any man, that he make amends to the uttermost of his power, &c."

The form of absolution in the English Prayer Book is omitted.

There is, however, in the American Prayer Book one especial direction in regard to Private Absolution, which is not found in the English Prayer Book. In the purely American Service for the Visitation of Prisoners this rubric occurs:

" Then shall the minister examine whether he repent him truly of his sins, exhorting him to a particular Confession of the sin for which he is condemned ; and upon Confession, he shall instruct him what satisfaction ought to be made to those whom he has offended thereby; and if he knoweth any combinations in wickedness, or any evil practices designed against others, let him be admonished to the utmost of his power to discover and prevent them."
"After his Confession the Priest shall declare to him the pardoning mercy of God, in the form which is used in the Communion Service."

The common argument adduced from these changes, by what are called moderate Churchmen, who would not deny Absolution in some shape; is that

Private Absolution is forbidden in the American Church, and that the special provision provided for it in the Visitation of Prisoners, is the exception that proves the rule.

Another view is taken by Mr. Hugh Davy Evans (Am. Edition of the Theoph. Amer. p. 149). He holds that the English Church encourages, but the American *discourages* private absolution. The exact force of the view of Mr. Evans it is difficult to see. Either the American Church forbids it, or she does not. If she permits it at all, she must permit it in all cases where it is right to administer it. To say that she discourages it then, is either equivalent to the statement that she forbids it, (with the one exception of the case of Visitation of Prisoners, when she commands it) or else it must mean that she permits private Absolution, whenever she permits private Confession. I purpose now to state the very great difficulties which the view that the Church *forbids* private absolution, involves.

1. The Preface to the Prayer Book states that "this Church is far from intending to depart from the Church of England in any essential point of doctrine, discipline or worship, or further than local circumstances require." The Church of England commands private absolution in certain cases; if the American Church forbids it, she either is not true to the principle above laid down, or private absolution is not an "essential point of discipline," which those who oppose it, will scarcely grant, any more than those who favour it.

2. It asserts the very grave principle, that omission implies prohibition. Private absolution is nowhere forbidden in the American Church, the two places where it is spoken of in the English Prayer Book are left out, and therefore it is argued that it is forbidden. Are those who maintain this view prepared to say that the Athanasian creed, the Magnificat, and the Nunc Dimittis are prohibited by the American Church, or even that their recitation or use at some special service is forbidden? When the Church catechism leaves out the word "elect," in the answer, "who sanctifies me and all the elect people of God," does she mean to prohibit the view that all baptized people are "elect." When she omits the rubric at the end of the marriage service in the English Prayer Book, "It is convenient that the new married persons should receive the holy Communion at the time of their marriage, or at the first opportunity after their marriage," does she mean to forbid this blessing to "new married persons." When she omits at the end of the service for the public Baptism of Infants, the solemn declaration:

"It is certain by God's word, that children which are baptized, dying before they commit actual sin, are undoubtedly saved,"

Does she mean to forbid this comforting assurance? When she leaves out the famous Black rubric at the end of the Communion office, does she mean to assert the opposite of that the Black rubric declares and means, when she requires her children to kneel at the Holy Communion, viz., "that adoration *is* intended and ought to be done, to the Sacramental bread and wine there bodily received," or to "a corporeal Presence of Christ's flesh and blood?" It is a dangerous thing to assert that omission means prohibition.

3. It does not take into account the exact character of the omissions, and if they mean prohibition, puts the Church, our mother, in a light which would be ludicrous were it not so pitiable.

a. In the exhortation to the Holy Communion in the American Prayer Book, if the penitent requires further "*comfort* or counsel" he is to go to God's minister and open his *grief*, that he may receive such *godly counsel and advice* as may tend, etc. In other words, according to this view, the penitent is to ask for two things (1) comfort, (2) counsel, and is to get nothing back but *counsel and advice*. The Priest is to say to him, I can give you counsel, but I cannot give you the comfort of assuring you that your sins are forgiven. In short, the penitent is to ask for bread and receive a stone.

b. According to this view, a man who has disgraced himself and his country, and is shut up in prison, provided he is penitent; can receive a blessing, which a sick man imprisoned in his own home by mortal illness, and needing and desiring the blessing just as much, because he is not a public criminal, can not have.

c Though the Church gives to her Priests the power to remit and retain sins in her ordination office, and never by any canon limits that power, save only as God limits it; she nevertheless, according to this view, with the solitary exception of the happy criminals, never permits a Priest to exercise this function of his office except in public worship; and one to whom the aweful trust is committed of guiding struggling souls to the Cross of Jesus, can never tell them they are forgiven, except with his surplice on, in the presence of a congregation.

d. This view makes the Church guilty of a piece of dissembling. In the visitation of the sick she requires the Priest to "examine" whether the sick person "repent him truly of his former sins," etc. This, of course, in some cases must involve confession. She then immediately after, in the very place where the absolution comes in the English Prayer Book, instructs the Priest to say over the sick person the prayer beginning, "O, most merciful God, who according to the multitude of Thy mercies dost so put away the sins of those who truly repent," etc. But this prayer is nothing more or less than the "reconciliation of a penitent near death" found in the Sacramentary of Gelasius, A. D. 494, with which the Church of God forgave her dying penitents, and which was used in theEnglish Church long before the indicative form of absolution was ever heard of. The American Church then on this view forbids private Absolution, while at the same time she surreptitiously absolves her dying penitents.

I submit that the difficulties of this view are so great that no plain, simplehearted man can possibly accept it, if there be any other reasonable explanation of the omissions. I venture to suggest that the most they can be shown clearly to prove, is that the Church thereby in consequence of the "local circumstances of the American Church" intended to give no approval to the mediæval form of absolution with the words, "I absolve thee," therein, as found in the English office for the visitation of the sick ; and that she did not in any sense intend to forbid private absolution, by some other form of words, not so liable to misconstruction.

———o———

V.

The following letter to Bishop Armitage was written early in June 1871. It is published because it explains the whole question referred to in the Defence. To it as one might expect the Bishop made no reply and the matter came to an end.

Rt. Rev. and Dear Bishop-

In the course of the conversation I had with you, you desired me to promise you, that I would not hear the confession of any Candidate for Holy Orders in the Diocese of Wisconsin without your permission, nor the Confession of any Candidate of any other Diocese, being a student of Nashotah, without the permission of the Bishop of such student.

Your action was based upon a correspondence which had passed between me and Dr. Adams, in which he had made certain accusations against me, and which, as I thought he had no right to make any complaint, I had courteously declined to respond to ; and upon a resolution passed by the Faculty of Nashotah which accuses me, "of an unauthorized and illegal intrusion upon the spiritual and pastoral care of the Candidates," in having allowed "several of the students, Candidates of this Diocese and of others," to resort to me "for private confession and absolution," without the knowledge and express sanction of their Bishops.

Permit me to say, first, that with the exception of two young men, one now in orders, who were for many years under my care, and whom I had trained from childhood, I have never heard the confession of but one Candidate of the Diocese of Wisconsin. He came to me because he was sent to me by his former Pastor, a clergyman whom you know and value ; but I felt it best for him to advise him, so soon as I knew you were making special exertions for your Candidates, to go to yourself for Spiritual assistance—advice which he was quite ready to follow.

I have heard the confessions of two persons who are Candidates from other Dioceses, and of two other persons, students at Nashotah, one of whom may possibly be a Candidate. One of these was a graduate of Racine College, who had been long under my care, and the others either sought me out, or were sent to me by others. One of these four was the student in the Preparatory Department at Nashotah, especially mentioned in Dr. Adams's letter Finding he desired to come to me, I went at once to Dr. Cole, told him of the Confessions I had heard, was assured by him that I had his consent to do good in that way; and with that consent freely given, I heard the confession of the youth in question.

I mention these facts not to excuse my hearing confessions of persons who have come to me, but to show that I have not sought out persons for this purpose, and thus been guilty of obtruding myself, or of offering my services, or as depreciating others, or setting up myself as a guide unbidden.

The question however is, as to whom, a person who by the means laid down in the Exhortation to the Communion office, cannot quiet his own conscience, "but requireth further comfort or counsel;" has a right to go for such comfort and counsel.

The words are "Let him come to me or *to some other minister of God's word*, and open his grief that he may receive" &c. I had supposed that there could be no question as to whether, a person troubled in conscience, in case he did not wish to go to his own Pastor, might not choose the clergyman to whom he would go. The words of the Prayer Book state it distinctly, I do not know how they can be twisted to mean anything else—and they are so I believe generally accepted.

Some twenty years ago the Rev. T.W. Allies, either then, or shortly afterwards a pervert to the Church of Rome, took the ground that a Priest not the Parish Priest of the Penitent, hearing a confession, had no jurisdiction. He was answered most conclusively by Dr 'Pusey in a letter entitled " The Church of England leaves her children free to whom to open their griefs." In this letter it was shown, that when the Church of England abolished compulsory confession, she also gave her children the further freedom to choose whom they would confide in.

The Church of Rome indeed, although she permits a multitude of exceptions, has a rule restricting her people; but I suppose the Nashotah Clergy, though sometimes accused (I am happy to think falsely) of Romanism, would hardly feel our clergy to be bound by them.

Among the numerous authorities for this view quoted by Dr. Pusey. I will merely adduce two.

Dean Comber says: "with us it [confession] is restricted to its primitive use; for we direct all men always to confess to God but some also to confess their faults and reveal their doubts to the Priest, especially in these three cases. (1) When we were disgusted with the guilt of some sin already committed, or (2) when we cannot conquer some lust or passion, or (3) when we are afflicted with any intricate scruple, particularly whether we may not be fit to receive this Blessed Sacrament or no. If any of these be our case then first we must choose prudently, preferring our own minister, if he be tolerably fitted, or else we *may elect another* that is prudent and pious, learned and juticious. One who may manage this weighty concern gravely and privately and despatch it wisely and fully to our satisfaction." Again Jeremy Taylor in the " Holy Dying" says: "Whether they be many or few that are sent to the sick person let the Curate of his Parish *or his own Confessor* be among them."

In Bishop Cosin's devotions which was, when I was a Tutor at Nashotah, and I fancy is still, the book of devotions recommended to the students, "among the precepts of the Church" is set down " To receive the blessed Sacrament of the Body and Blood of Christ, with frequent devotion and three times a year at least, of which times Easter to be always one And for better preparation thereunto, as occasion is, to disburthen and quiet our consciences of those sins that may gieeve us, or scruples that may trouble us, to a learned and discreet Priest and from him to receive advice and the benefit of absolution." Is it wonderful that some of the students of Nashotah should have wished to practise what so great a Bishop commends, and what the authorized book of devotions at Nashotah enjoins. Nor is there any authority for supposing as I heard you say some one had suggested, (even had it been retained in our American Prayer Book), thathe word ":discreet'' in the English Prayer Book limited the authority to one especially set apart to bear confessions. There is no authority for such an interpretation. No such persons were ever appointed in the Church of England, and while there are visitation articles of Bishops which refer to the subject of confession, including men like Andrewes, and Overall, and at least one canon since the Reformation (in 1603) has been passed upon the same subject, the authority of the Priest has never, either in England or in this Country, in this respect been limited.

The question next arises. Is a Candidate for Holy Orders, in the matter in question, in a different position from any other layman. There is so far as I can discover no possible interpretation of any canon, law or provision of the Church, by which a Candidate for Holy Orders is deprived of the privilege if he wishes to use it. A lay man is free to go to whom he will. A Deacon and a Priest who are much more closely bound to a Bishop than a Candidate have the same freedom, nor does the Candidate ever surrender his right.

I think it eminently desirable that the relations of a Bishop to his Candidates should be such as would always induce a Candidate to go to him for such assistance. I am happy to know that you endeavour to make them so. Every loyal Presbyter would do what I have already done, in the case of the one Candidate from this Diocese I have mentioned: and thus do the utmost to assist the Bishop in his efforts. Such a course I should always under similar circumstances feel it right to pursue. You yourself appeared to feel that in the case of some youth brought up as it were by me, with whom there had been long personal and pastoral relations an exception might properly be made. What I have written applies equally well to Candidates from other Dioceses attending an Institution purporting to be general. Such an

Institution could—disregarding the Prayer Book—make a law that no student should go to confession to any one but its own officers. It could enforce the rule by pains and penalties. Such a rule would seem for a multitude of reasons, quite independent of its opposition to the Prayer Book, to be a foolish one. It often happens that a student cannot go for Spiritual purposes to those who are engaged in instructing him. But if Nashotah were to make such a rule, and a student were to enter there knowing that such a rule existed, I should be the last person to encourage him in disobedience. Even without such a rule one would be most careful to assist the authorities even where a wish only were expressed, as far at least as possible.

If again the Presbyters at Nashotah were so to influence their students, that they should at once be drawn to them for spiritual purposes, every faithful Priest would feel like assisting them in this blessed work. One would be most careful still further not to do any thing which might disturb the relations of a Candidate to his Bishop. But with these limitations and reservations the Candidate has the right to disburthen his soul to whom he will, and any Priest has the right to hear him.

I write these things, my dear Bishop, as they are presented to my mind, to beg of you not to issue any command to me upon the subject nor to ask of me any promise. I think you ought not to. 1st, Because by saying that under no conceivable circumstances I, and so any other Priest, must hear the confession of a candidate for Holy Orders in this Diocese, or of any other candidate, you are limiting the lawful rights of Candidates, and that in their highest and most important relations, i. e. to their own souls. 2d. You are deterring persons from becoming Candidates in this Diocese and especially from going to Nashotah. 3d, You are so far, without trial suspending me and others also, from the legitimate exercise of one function of the ministry, a function too rarely used I fear. Further, by asking me to promise I will obey such a command, you place me in the position either of disobeying you, or else that I should be forced to do two things, 1st, that, being one who from circumstances has done and is doing more, than perhaps any other single person in the Northwest, in directing the minds of young men to the Candidateship; I nevertheless deliberately surrender their rights ; and 2d, which is more important, that by my own consent, I should give up one of the duties of the office I have solemnly pledged myself to carry out.

There is another reason which I feel I have a right to urge. For nearly seventeen years, first as Tutor in Ecclesiastical History at Nashotah, then as head of the preparatory department, then for nearly twelve years as President of Racine College, I have been laboring to build up a high tone amongst those preparing to become Candidates for Holy Orders. You know—what from the day I came to this Diocese I have known, that there has been, and is much, need.

I have been struggling to make those whom I have had under my charge what they ought to be, and by God's blessing I have, I trust, been successful and am yearly more and more so. High scholarship—gentlemanly bearing, true honour, loving penitence and high-hearted devotion, for these I have labored. My effort to assist a few struggling souls who came legitimately under my influence and without my seeking, has been a part of this effort. I had no reason to suppose that it would receive a formal censure from Nashotah. It had *the express approval of the President and Pastor.* That it has received a censure, at once discourteous and ungrateful, I must bear patiently ; but this I beg—under these circumstances—do not allow yourself, my Bishop, who ought lovingly to sustain me, to be made a scourge, where with a fellow-Presbyter may the more heavily afflict me. In the wider interests of the whole church something more may be said. Not every Bisnop is fitted to be the spiritual adviser of his candidates ; not every Bishop is willing to be so. Even supposing the Bishop to be all that he ought to be, willing and earnest, one can easily imagine circumstances in which the candidate could not go to him ; and there might be other cases in which a candidate would naturally prefer a Pastor, who had trained him from youth, guided him through boynood and early manhood, directed his attention to the ministry, and been to him by God's blessing more than any one else.

Believe it my dear Bishop, in so sacred a matter the largest liberty with a candidate, and the broadest toleration within the limits of the Prayer-Book to a Presbyter, will be the wisest policy, as well as tend most to the salvation of souls.

I am, affectionately your Son in Christ,

JAMES DE KOVEN.

———o———

VI.

THE PRAYERS IN THE TREASURY OF DEVOTION.

The prayers quoted by Dr. Adams from the Treasury of Devotion were as follows pp. 10, 245 and 247:

INTERCESSION;

Almighty and Everlasting God, Who hast promised to hear the petitions of those who ask in Thy Son's Name, I commend unto Thee my Parents, my Brothers, and Sisters, my Wife or Husband, my Children and Godchildren, and all my Relations, Friends, Dependants, and those for whom I have been asked to pray. Let Thy Fatherly hand, I beseech Thee, ever be over them, let Thy Holy Spirit ever be with them, and so lead them in the knowledge and obedience of Thy word, that in the end they may obtain everlasting life. Pity, O

Lord, and have mercy upon all men, for Jesus Christ's sake, Who with Thee and the Holy Ghost, liveth and reigneth, ever One God, world without end. Amen.

May the intercessions of the holy Mother of God, of the Prophets, of the holy Apostles, of the Martyrs, help me! May all the Saints and Elect of God pray for me, that I may be worthy with them to possess the Kingdom of God. Amen.

May the holy Angels, especially my own Guardian, keep watch around me throughout this day, to protect me against the assaults of the evil one, to suggest to me holy thoughts, to defend me against all dangers, to lead me in the perfect way of peace, and to bring me safe, at length, to my home in Heaven.

MEMORIAL OF THE BLESSED VIRGIN.

Antiphon; The Holy Ghost shall come upon thee, and the power of the Highest shall overshadow Thee : therefore also that holy thing which shall be born of thee shall be called the Son of God.

V Blessed art thou among women.
R And blessed is the fruit of thy womb.

LET US PRAY.

O God, Who in the overshadowing of the Holy Ghost wert conceived in the womb of a human mother, still a Virgin, who gave Thee birth and nurtured Thee ; and Who, laid in her bosom, wert presented in the Temple to the Father an Offering and Sacrifice for us ; grant, we beseech Thee, that we, sharing Thy nature, one flesh and one spirit with Thee, a new creation in Thyself, may be made like unto Thee in all things ; and, living according to Thy holy Will, may be presented a living sacrifice, holy, acceptable to God through Thy merits and perpetual intercession ; to Whom be glory forever. Amen.

O Lord Jesus Christ, born of the Virgin Mary ; teach me to reverence Thy Holy Mother, according to Thy will. Thou didst send Thy Angel to salute her as highly favoured, and blessed among women, meet to be the mother of God by the operation of the Holy Ghost. Thou wast subject unto her, and didst commit her to Thy beloved disciple, saying, "Behold thy mother." With Thy Angel, I would give her praise ; with Thyself love her ; with Thine Apostle honour her. Howsoever Thy Saints have profited through her intercessions, may I in like manner profit; through Thee, Who with the Father and the Holy Ghost, livest and reignest, One God, world without end. Amen,

OF A DOCTOR;

Antiphon. Light eternal shall shine on Thy Saints, O Lord, and length of days. Alleluia.

V Rejoice in the Lord, O ye Righteous.
R For it becometh well the just to be thankful. Alleluia.

LET US PRAY.

O God, Who willedst Thy blessed servant, Saint N., to be an illustrious Teacher for the instruction and edification of Thy Holy Church; grant, we beseech Thee, that as on earth he taught us the way of life, so now he may plead and pray for us in Heaven ; through Jesus Christ our Lord. Amen.

OF A VIRGIN AND MARTYR.

Antiphon. When the Bridegroom came, they that were ready went in with Him to the marriage. Alleluia.

V The virgins that be her fellows.
R Shall bear her company.

LET US PRAY.

Almighty and Everlasting God, Who choosest the weak things of the world to confound the wise : mercifully grant that we, who celebrate the Festival of Thy holy servant, Saint M., Virgin (and Martyr), may also enjoy the advantage of her prayers in our behalf before Thee ; through Jesus Christ our Lord. Amen.

The Roman doctrine of the Invocation of Saints involves two things, first, that we may pray to the Saints, secondly, that they can directly help us. Neither of these views are to be found in these prayers in the Treasury of Devotion. They are every one of them *Prayers to God, not prayers to the Saints.* They do not *pray that the saints may help us,* but only that we may be profited by their prayers to God. In other words that *He may help us* because of their prayers. They are exactly in the line of the Collect for St. Michael's Day in the Prayer Book, when we pray to God to give us the succour and defence of the Holy Angels; with the difference of course, that such Christians believe of the angels, that they are " ministering spirits sent forth to minister unto them who shall be heirs of salvation," which may not be true of the Saints.

Perhaps there is no greater instance of unfairness in controversy than the assertion in the *Church Journal* of Feb. 26th, that the Prayers to the Saints and angels in Mr. Orby Shipley's " Invocation of Saints and Angels" "are no more than can be found in a book edited by Mr. Carter of Clewer

—62—

"*The Treasury of Devotion*," a book given by advanced clergymen very commonly to those whom they spiritually "direct" &c."

Either the Editor had never examined Mr. Shipley's Book or else he has ventured to rely on the supposed ignorance of his readers for an assertion he cannot prove. The Treasury of Devotion only contains prayers to God for the intercession of the Saints. Mr. Shipley's book is full of Litanies and Prayers to the Saints themselves, and whatever may be thought of the latter, to state that the former are like them, is to make a grave misstatement.

For myself I heartily subscribe to the language of Dr. Pusey (letter to the Bishop of London p. 101.) though I am not sufficiently familiar with Mr. Shipley's book, to know whether it has such expressions in it as are here condemned.

"It (the Invocation of Saints) however it may be explained by Roman Catholic controversalists, to be no more than asking the prayers of members of Christ, now in the flesh ; still, in use, it is plainly more ; for no one would ask those in the flesh 'to protect us from the enemy' ' receive us in the hour of death' 'lead us to the joy of heaven,' 'may thy (the blessed virgin) abundant love cover the multitude of sins,' ' and to the mind which asketh thee give the gift of graces,' or use any of the direct prayers for graces which God alone can bestow, which are common in R. C. devotions to the Blessed Virgin. No one can look uncontroversially at such occasional addresses, as there are to martyrs in the 4th century (and these chiefly prayers at their tombs through their intercession for miraculous aid from God,) and such books as the 'glories of Mary, the 'Month of Mary,' and say, that the character of the modern reliance on, and invocation of Saints, was that of the Ancient Church." But such just criticisms do not apply in any sense to the Prayers in the "Treasury of Devotion"

Of them the words of Bishop Andrewes, than whom no one has written more earnestly against the Invocation of Saints, are evidently true.

"While the Fathers were fully persuaded that the Saints (no matter where they were,) still were interested in our behalf, and in their way kindly prayed for us; so far at least as that they (the Fathers) could be aided by this cooperation of theirs, and by their intercessions and services. Yet it was not from the Saints themselves that this was solicited, but always from God. *But to ask God to be propitious to us at their request, this request of them* IS NOT AN INVOCATION OF THEM, BUT OF GOD. (Responsio ad. Card. Bellarmine Lib. Angl. Cath. Theo. p. 60.)

Thus speaks this great Bishop who seems to have written almost as much to the confusion of my accusers, as of Cardinal Bellarmine.

The "*Anima Christi*"which is found in the Treasury of Devotion, was also an especial point of attack of Dr. Adams. He omitted however to tell his hearers that Bishop Andrewes himself whose works are spoken of in "Principles not men" as one of the "text Books" of high churchmen as distinguished from the "advanced," made use of this prayer with the following alterations.

PRAYER OF IGNATIUS LOYOLA.	PRAYER OF BISHOP ANDREWES.
Anima Christi Sanctifica me	Anima Christi Sanctifica me
Corpus Christi Salva me	Corpus Christi conforta me
Sanguis Christi inebria me	Sanguis Christi redime me
Aqua Latetis Christi lava me	Aqua Christi ablue me
Passio Christi conforta me	Livor Christi sava me
O bono Jesu exandi me	Sudor Christi refrigera me
Jntra tua vulnera absconde me, &c.	Vulnus Christi absconde me

[Devotions of Bishop Andrewes (p. 163 Lib. of Ang. Cath. Theo.)]

TRANSLATION.

IGNATIUS.	BISHOP ANDREWES.
Soul of Christ sanctify me	Soul of Christ sanctify me
Body of Christ save me	Body of Christ strengthen me

Blood of Christ inebriate me	Blood of Christ ransom me
Water from the side of Christ cleanse me	Water (from the side of) Christ cleanse me
Passion of Christ comfort me	Bruises of Christ heal me
O good Jesu hear me	Sweat of Christ refresh me
Hide me within Thy wounds &c·	Wound of Christ hide me

The use of the Anima Christi by Bishop Andrewes is the more remarkable, because having been born but a few years after the death of Ignatius, he must have gone out of his way to get it. It is he who introduced it into the English Church.* It did not come to him as it has to us after long centuries of use. Bishop Andrewes has indeed altered the one word which Dr. Adams dwelt upon, the word "inebriate". Preferring myself the word "ransom" it must be remembered that there is very high authority for the use of "inebriate." The language is to be found as being employed in Holy Scripture, in St. Cyprian, St. Ambrose, St. Augustine, Eusebius, Origen, St. Cyril of Jerusalem, St. Gregory Nyssen, St. Athanasius, and Theodoret. Should any one wish to look up the passages, the references can all be found in Dr. Pusey's letter to the Bishop of London p. 145.

The word "inebriate" in the figurative language which the fathers used simply means that by the Blood of Christ, spiritually given us in the Holy Communion, we are *born out of and above ourselves.* The soul "was athirst for God," it "hungered and thirsted after righteousness," it was "to drink of the river of Thy pleasures." "And thus words as "inebriating" or those of the like meaning which sound strangely in our ears, who have it is to be feared so little of the joy of the ancient church, do declare the highest mystery of Christian joy. For man may be out of himself either by being above or below himself; and in their highest degree the outward semblance may in either case be the same." (See Dr. Pusey's letter, p. 154 and 155.)

It must also be noted that the verse of the 23d Psalm, "Thy cup shall be full" is in the Latin version of the English Prayer Book authorized in the time of Queen Elizabeth, 1560, "*calix meus* INEBRIANS *quam præclarus est*" and in the latest Latin version of the Book of Common Prayer that of Messrs. Bright & Medd the same phrase following the Vulgate is used.

No one of course is compelled to use a Prayer like the "Anima Christi." If the word "inebriate" does not please him he can surely alter it, but to condemn a book of Devotions on that account, much more one who happens to give it away, seems to be the height of absurdity.

---

* May it not have been brought from Spain at the time of the visit of Prince Charles (1623) who was accompanied by Dr. Wren, when Bishop Andrewes was Bishop of Winchester.

ERRATA.

Page 25. To the second paragraph of the quotation from Thorndike, the following should be added :

"Grant that there may be question, whether it be a just occasion or not ; certainly supposing it came to a custom in the Church presently to do that which is always due to be done, you suppose the question determined. This is that which I stand upon ; the matter being such as it is, supposing the custom of the Church to have determined it, it shall be so far from an act of idolatry, that it shall be the duty of a good Christian. Therefore. not supposing the Church to have determined it, though for some occasions, (whereof more are possible than it is possible for one to imagine) it may become offensive and not presently due, yet can it never become an act of idolatry ; so long as Christianity is that which it is, and he that does it professes himself a Christian."

Page 44. The quotation from the Collect for St. Michael and all Angels should read :

"Grant that as Thy Holy Angels always do Thee service in Heaven, so by Thy appointment they may succour and defend us on earth."

www.ingramcontent.com/pod-product-compliance
Lightning Source LLC
Chambersburg PA
CBHW021512090426
42739CB00007B/575